The Economics of E-commerce

The Economics of E-commerce

A STRATEGIC GUIDE TO UNDERSTANDING AND
DESIGNING THE ONLINE MARKETPLACE

Nir Vulkan

Princeton University Press
Princeton and Oxford

Published by Princeton University Press,
41 William Street, Princeton, New Jersey 08540

In the United Kingdom: Princeton University Press,
3 Market Place, Woodstock, Oxfordshire OX20 1SY

Library of Congress Cataloging-in-Publication Data

Vulkan, Nir.
    The economics of e-commerce: a strategic guide to
understanding and designing the online marketplace / Nir
Vulkan.
        p. cm.
    Includes bibliographical references and index.

    ISBN 0-691-08906-X (cloth : alk. paper)

1. Electronic commerce. I. Title: Economics of e-commerce.
II. Title.

    HF5548.32.V85 2003
    381'.1—dc21   2002192494

This book has been composed in Stone Serif and Stone Sans
by Stephen I. Pargeter, Banbury, Oxfordshire, UK

Printed on acid-free paper. ∞

www.pupress.princeton.edu

Printed in the United States of America

10 9 8 7 6 5 4 3 2 1

In loving memory of my father, Uzi

Contents

Preface

This book builds on research I have carried out over the last four years into the economics of electronic commerce. Towards the end of 1996 many leading computer scientists designing agents and e-commerce applications became interested in using game theory. One team from the University of London approached the economics department where I was completing my PhD, asking for advice on how to apply game theory to automated negotiations. I already had Bachelors and Masters degrees in computer science, and was keen to get involved. My work on automated negotiations quickly grew to become a more general interest in the e-commerce phenomenon. There then followed four fascinating years of work on e-commerce with computer scientists, economists, start-up companies, management consultants and the e-commerce research team in the Hewlett–Packard laboratories.

As my e-commerce work progressed, it soon became clear that there were two different research agendas. The first was the use of microeconomic analysis to gain an understanding of the value of various e-commerce technologies and Internet-based trading mechanisms. In the period between 1997 and 1999 e-commerce companies were the darlings of investors. Blinded by fantastic market capitalization rates, little attention was paid to the answers provided by start-up companies to questions such as who will pay for what and why. Often, startups would say something like "this application will save consumers an average of $10 and therefore they will be willing to pay $5 for it". While such statements were often true, they tended to ignore what I call the "total game", for example the response of sellers to applications that empower buyers. For instance, sellers can (and do) block access to their sites to many e-commerce applications, or even use the same technology for a different purpose. In the long run, only business models based on sound economic propositions—which take into account the "total game"—will survive and flourish. And that is where microeconomic analysis is essential.

The second research agenda was centered on the use of game theory for designing and running e-commerce applications. The early attempts of computer scientists to use game theory in automated negotiations fall into this category. In particular, there was—and still is—huge interest in auctions for buying and selling almost anything. The success of eBay (and to a lesser extent Priceline.com) made auctions familiar and popular with consumers. Moreover, they triggered consumer appetite for new methods of buying and selling goods. On the business side, companies such as Ariba, CommerceOne and FreeMarkets heavily promoted the use of auctions in business-to-business transactions. The wave of largely successful mobile phone auctions in the United States and Europe also contributed strongly to the notion that game theory is a useful theory in designing economic institutions.

Game theory is the study of the interactions between rational decision-makers. It is formal and is based largely on mathematical modeling. It is perfectly suited for designing e-commerce applications because of the formal nature of the rules that govern the interactions between participants. The second part of the book is therefore a reference guide to the principles of economic engineering in the context of e-commerce: how economic analysis—and game theory in particular—can be used to help design efficient e-commerce applications.

The first years of co-operation between game theorists, economists and computer scientists led to an explosion of research in this area—so much so that in the first world conference in game theory (held in Bilbao in the summer of 2000), there were almost as many computer scientists as economists. In my opinion this research has only just begun. The computer scientists working in this area belong mainly to a field of computer science known as artificial intelligence (AI).[1] It is an interesting

---

[1] Interestingly, AI—which was big in the 1980s and vanished in the 1990s—is now making a comeback. In March 2002 *The Economist* wrote: "Large companies are also using the term [AI] ... Microsoft announced a "breakthrough application that enlists

fact that AI and economics have had many overlapping inter-ests over the years. John von Neuman's pioneering work laid the foundations for modern AI as well as modern game theory. Along the same lines, Herbert Simon's work on rationality and bounded rationality greatly influenced research in both fields. It is therefore not surprising that we find ourselves today in a situation where researchers from both fields are working together in pursuit of what may become one of the more important technological changes of modern life.

In the short term, computer science is likely to benefit more from this cooperation, because economic wisdom on the effi-ciency of systems consisting of self-interested agents can be directly applied to most e-commerce applications. In addition, the economic methodology, which stresses the importance of looking for the underlying incentives of participants, can pro-vide important insights into automated negotiations and electronic trade. But in the long term, economists also have much to gain from this joint adventure. By focusing on what is essentially an application of economic theory and mechanism design to automated environments, we can learn about the use-fulness of our theories and intuitions.

HOW TO USE THIS BOOK

Although this book is based on recent research, it is essentially a textbook, and should be read as such. It is designed primarily for MBA students. The course is intended for those students who are likely to implement e-commerce in the organization for which they work, or through work as consultants, or for those who are considering starting their own Internet business or working for such a start-up.

The book can be used as a text for an MBA elective. In Oxford this elective is titled "advanced e-commerce". To cover the whole book, a minimum of 15–20 teaching hours are required. It is essential from my experience that students have already taken a basic course in microeconomics (for example managerial economics), because otherwise it is easy to get "bogged down" in trying to grasp basic economic concepts. However, it should be possible to cover the material without being too formal—most of the intuitions are straightforward

---

the power of artificial intelligence to help users manage mobile communications. ...
Sony also unabashedly uses the term AI."

and could be explained using basic diagrams and examples. The book can also be used in more "general purpose" microeconomics course for MBA as a source of examples and applications of the theory.

Some of the chapters are more difficult than others. In particular, chapters 3 and 4 are more theoretical, and it might be advisable to dedicate more than one lecture to each of these. Alternatively, it would be possible to cover only parts of these chapters. Chapter 5 is more general and can be used either as an introduction to the second part of the book, or as a topic on its own. In the latter case it will be useful to supplement the reading, for example with material from Milgrom and Robert's *Economics, Organization and Management* (1998). Migrom and Roberts include many useful discussions and examples of incentive contracts and economic engineering. The remaining three chapters of this book—6, 7 and 8—are, in my experience, relatively straightforward to teach, and there are many examples that can be used to illustrate the material covered in these chapters.

The book is also suitable for undergraduate and graduate economics students. When teaching graduate students it may be useful to suggest that students read the actual research papers referred to in the text.

The book covers research other than my own, but it is heavily biased toward my own work. It might be a good idea to supplement the reading with other texts, particularly with the excellent "Information Rules" by Shapiro and Varian (1999), to give students a more comprehensive view of the economic issues in e-commerce.

Acknowledgments

The book is centered on my research over the last four years. During this time I have had the pleasure of working with a number of other researchers in this area. In particular, my research with Ken Binmore, Tuomas Sandholm, Zvika Neeman and Chris Preist is described in various places in the book. It was a great experience working with each of them. I am particularly grateful to Ken, who also provided helpful comments on an early version of various chapters.

In writing the book, I was greatly assisted by Eleanor Scott, my research assistant, who helped compile many of the examples used in the book. Romesh Vaitilingam provided valuable help in organizing the book, and I am grateful for his many useful suggestions. I am also in debt to my editor, Richard Baggaley for his support throughout the ups and downs of this project.

Finally, many thanks to my wife Fiona for her patience, and for looking after our babies in the long evenings while I was writing this book. I dedicate this book in memory of my father, Uzi Vulkan, who instilled in me the love of learning and science.

The Economics of E-commerce

Chapter 1

Introduction and Overview

The phenomenal growth of the Internet since the mid-1990s is an unprecedented event in the history of information and communications technology. The Internet, essentially a collection of computer networks linked by cable and satellite, which started off connecting four supercomputers, today links more than 300 million people in 170 countries. And the rate of Internet traffic continues to grow rapidly.

The Internet has already fundamentally changed the way many individuals and organizations think about and perform their work. Electronic commerce—the conduct of business activities electronically via digital media—is now part of everyday business. And despite the sharp falls in the share prices of many 'dotcoms' since early 2000, e-commerce is still likely to have a major and *lasting* effect on most forms of economic activities.

This is true for the interactions of businesses both with consumers and with other businesses. On the business-to-business (B2B) side, web-based procurement systems, online business auctions and electronic negotiations are already commonplace in the interactions of large to medium-sized businesses with their suppliers and clients.[1] On the consumer side, the Internet is emerging as a significant medium for buying and selling certain goods, such as books, computer software and hardware, music CDs and airline tickets.

Advances in web-based technologies further support the growth of e-commerce. In particular, automation and delega-

---

[1] On October 5, 2002, *The Economist* ran a story "Life after dotcom death", which began with the sentence; "If you think B2B market places are dead, read on".

1

tion technologies—known variously as intelligent or smart 'agents', 'shopping bots' or 'bidding elves'—are likely to have a considerable effect on the future of e-commerce. These software programs make it possible, for example, for consumers to conduct automated searches and price comparisons, and for online sellers to know the identity of visiting consumers, access background information on them in real-time and adjust their prices and offerings accordingly. The technologies can even make decisions on behalf of individuals, negotiate with other programs and participate in online markets.

Much of the economic value of e-commerce arises from this kind of automation. The opportunities to use the Internet for business and comparison shopping are increased significantly by technologies that can take the place of activities that were previously done manually, especially those that were most costly in terms of data and working hours. And e-commerce, particularly automated e-commerce, creates new economic value not only by making business processes easier, but also by opening up new possibilities for market interactions.

That is the issue at the heart of this book. The aim is to provide an understanding of the added economic value of e-commerce applications for readers searching for "e-commerce solutions". These might include e-commerce strategists and business managers in corporations, designers of new applications—whether online retailers, B2B marketplaces, negotiation technologies, auction websites or electronic exchanges—and potential investors in these enterprises.

As the rise and fall in the valuations of the first wave of e-commerce companies show, promises of profits at some vague point in the future are no longer going to be sufficient. Only business models based on sound economic propositions will survive and flourish. And that is where economic analysis is essential. This book provides the reader with the tools to understand and evaluate the underlying economic propositions of the wide range of actual and potential e-commerce businesses. And it demonstrates how the tools can be used to assess a variety of existing applications.

The first part of the book investigates the economic value of both consumer and business e-commerce applications, using the tools of economic analysis to explore key questions about the variety of trading mechanisms on the Internet. For example, are electronic markets likely to be more or less competitive than 'bricks-and-mortar' markets? And what are the pros and cons of dynamic pricing, where sellers price their offerings according to the identity of each individual consumer? The goal is to understand the advantages of online trading mechanisms and the choices of individuals and organizations over which mechanism to use and when.

Chapter 2 lays out the basic tools of economic analysis that can be used to evaluate e-commerce applications, notably the assumption of rationality, game theory and the concept of equilibrium. The guiding principle is that, to understand the way electronic markets—indeed any markets—work, it is essential to have an overarching framework of analysis.

This demands, first, a basic intuition of what incentives determine economic behavior, and the only reasonable one to use is rationality, i.e. that people (and software programs operating on their behalf) act in their own best interests. Second, it requires a way of thinking about how economic interactions take place across the whole market place; game theory is a very effective tool. And finally, it needs a "solution", some means of predicting and assessing the potential outcome or outcomes of all those interactions, and that comes from the concept of equilibrium.

Chapter 3 surveys e-commerce for consumers, focusing in particular on the economic implications of Internet technologies for prices and product offerings, and for competition between firms. There are two key questions: what are the incentives for consumers and retailers to trade online; and is it buyers or sellers who benefit the most? Relatively simple economic analysis can clarify the economic proposition underlying many consumer e-commerce technologies, notably "ShopBots", i.e. virtual robots that scan the web for price and product information on behalf of consumers and retailers, and 'personalization technologies', which provide retailers and marketing companies with an enormous amount of consumer-specific data.

Shopping bots, for example, reduce the search costs of consumers virtually to zero since the software program does all the searching. At first sight, this might suggest that markets will become more competitive and prices will fall, at least those for homogeneous goods like books, CDs and software. But economic analysis casts some doubt on this view, and there is evidence that, although the prices of some goods are cheaper on the Internet, loyalty and branding still play a major role in the electronic retailing industry.

Economics sheds light on the real relationship between consumer search power and the pricing strategies of online sellers, especially the new opportunities the latter have, using personalization technologies, to tailor both prices and products to individual consumers. Sellers can now take advantage of the vast array of data on their customers to treat them as individuals, employing such practices as price discrimination, product differentiation, 'one-to-one' marketing and mass customization. Chapter 3 addresses the incentives for both sellers and consumers to engage with each other using these technologies and marketing strategies.

Chapter 4 provides an overview of B2B e-commerce, focusing in particular on the economic advantages of trading through e-commerce and comparing the pros and cons of the three main forms of electronic markets. In broad terms, firms can trade online via 'one-to-one' or direct negotiations; by participating in 'one-to-many' auctions; or through 'many-to-many' exchanges, where there are many potential buyers and sellers at any given time.

The volume of business e-commerce is estimated to be nearly ten times as large as that of consumer e-commerce. Most companies now use the Internet in one way or another to trade with their suppliers and corporate customers. Large parts of the supply chain are automated using e-commerce. And auctions are commonplace, as are web-based markets for many commodities, like steel and metal.

Chapter 4 provides a framework with which to understand the economic value of these business electronic markets. There are two key questions: what is the added economic value from switching to trading with other businesses from offline to online; and what is the preferable online trading mechanism; that is, how do firms choose the most profitable way to trade online? Economic analysis reveals how web-based markets—online auctions and electronic exchanges—can overcome the inefficiencies often associated with direct negotiations.

If part I of this book is about evaluating existing e-commerce applications, part II is about how to make things better. Economic engineering—the design of market mechanisms that encourage desirable economic outcomes—is certainly not a new invention, but the opportunities for practicing it have increased dramatically with the growth of e-commerce. The public seems to have acquired an appetite for trying out new ways of buying and selling. Managers understand that proper economic engineering can make all the difference to their businesses. And the pressure toward trading electronically and further automation of the supply chain increases, because no one wants to be left out. It is no longer acceptable for managers not to know the advantages and disadvantages of auctions, say, or price discrimination.

The second part of the book is therefore a reference guide to the principles of economic engineering in the context of e-commerce: how economic analysis—and game theory in particular—can be used to help design efficient e-commerce applications.

It has been said that economists are forever theorizing about how they could make the world more efficient if only they were given a chance. Over the last ten years or so, they have finally had that chance. For example, the U.S. Federal Communications Commission invited a number of game theorists to design its telecommunications auctions. These turned out to be a huge success, bringing in revenues far greater than originally expected. Other countries, including the U.K., followed suit, employing game theorists to design large-scale auctions in order to maximize the government's revenue from licencing state-owned and natural resources.

Economic engineering is of course much more general than auction design. It is a set of tools for designing the rules that govern any interactions between individuals and firms. Over the last three decades, rapid progress in game theory has brought the subject to an engineering-like state, where a large number of well understood mechanisms can be prescribed for given sets of circumstances. Electronic markets are a particularly good place to apply this theory, because the interactions between participants are already regulated by the communication protocols of the software. They may as well be regulated by a well designed protocol, which, by setting the 'rules of the game' appropriately, provides participants with the right incentives leading to efficient outcomes.

Chapter 5 sets out the basic principles of market engineering and its uses for e-commerce. Game theory can be used to consider the possible implications of various sets of rules, such as auctions and exchange, on the behavior of self-interested participants. On the basis of these conclusions, it is then possible to select mechanisms that ensure the efficiency of many types of e-commerce application.

Chapter 6 describes how ideas from the theory of negotiation can be used to resolve potential conflicts between participants in e-commerce applications. Negotiations lie at the heart of almost all e-commerce scenarios: buyers and sellers bargain for a price, companies negotiate the terms of agreement, and so on. In fact, a certain degree of conflict of interest is inevitable in most e-commerce applications (because of the nature of inter-actions between self-interested economic actors), and the parties involved must use some form of negotiation to resolve it.

Economic analysis takes the view that the choice of protocol (or the "rules of the game") will typically affect the behavior of participants. For example, someone (or a software program act-ing on a person's behalf) who is capable of making a credible "take-it-or-leave-it" offer is typically in a good bargaining posi-tion (*paradoxically* because they refuse to bargain). The designers of e-commerce systems must therefore take account of the strategic considerations of participants, especially in one-to-one bargaining situations, where these considerations are particularly significant. Chapter 6 reviews the theory and appli-cations, and describes a number of new technologies designed specifically for e-commerce applications that involve one-to-one bargaining.

Chapter 7 deals with auctions, clear winners of the e-com-merce phenomena. Consumer web-based auction houses like eBay.com involve trade worth millions of dollars every day. Businesses in large numbers are incorporating online auctions into their transactions. And Microsoft's release of an auction component in its e-commerce server will probably cause an increasing number of website developers to consider online auctions as part of their e-commerce solutions. By using an auc-tion—instead of committing in advance to a fixed price—the seller is able to charge prices that reflect what buyers are willing to pay. This practice can, in many cases, increase the profits of the seller considerably.

Auctions are also an effective way of resolving the 'one-to-many' bargaining problem so that the seller does not need to negotiate with each of the potential buyers separately. This is particularly true for e-commerce, since the Internet can support only a limited amount of communication at any given time. Chapter 7 reviews the basic principles behind auction theory and describes a number of common auction types. It also describes a number of e-commerce auction technologies.

Chapter 8 explores 'many-to-many' negotiations. This is a common set-up for trading in most commodities, where at any given stage there are many buyers and sellers.

The chapter explains how exchanges operate, how they are created and the incentives of participants to join them. It also provides designers of e-commerce exchanges with the basic theoretical tools to create and maintain such markets.

The chapter begins by discussing how goods and services can be standardized and describes the experience of a number of exchanges that struggle to standardize their offerings. It then discusses how exchanges work. Specifically, we examine what it means to set clearing prices and what affects this is likely to have on the market.

A key factor in determining the success of the exchange is its ability to provide liquidity. The chapter explains what exactly liquidity is and who provides it. It shows that industry consortiums are most likely to succeed in the long run because of their ability to bring enough liquidity to the market.

Finally, the chapter discusses the possibility of automating trading, by providing traders with software agents. Agents reduce the cost of trading, and increase its speed. These affects can increase trading volume, market efficiency and the profits made by the exchange. But traders need to trust their agents. The chapter describes Hewlett–Packard's "Jester" experiments on the human–agent interface in exchange trading, and draws conclusions for the future use of such a technology.

The book ends with a case study of electronic communications networks (ECNs) and the affect they had on security trading in the United States in the second part of the 1990s.

PART I

EVALUATING E-COMMERCE APPLICATIONS

Chapter 2

E-commerce and the Tools of Economic Analysis

The latter half of the 1990s and the early years of the new millennium have witnessed an enormous growth in interest in the possibilities of e-commerce. But much of the hype has focused on specific applications, such as the success (in terms of media profile if not business profitability) of particular "early mover" companies like Amazon. Relatively little consideration has gone into a systematic overview of the economic development of e-commerce, thinking carefully through the incentives and interactions of buyers and sellers across the whole electronic marketplace.

But economic analysis is a powerful way of thinking about the business world, and this chapter begins to make a case for using economics as an essential tool for understanding e-commerce. It lays out the basic tools of economic analysis that can be used to evaluate e-commerce applications, notably the assumption of rationality, game theory and the concept of equilibrium. The guiding principle is that, to understand the way electronic markets—indeed, any markets—work, it is essential to have an overarching framework of analysis. Such a framework will be of great value to software designers, business managers and investors in e-commerce applications.

THE PHENOMENAL GROWTH OF E-COMMERCE

The single most important force behind the phenomenal growth of e-commerce is the increased access to the Internet. The Internet itself, however, is only the *medium* for the services using it, like e-mail, the World Wide Web and e-commerce. No single organization or government owns the Internet—although the telecoms companies own much of its backbone—and consequently it is much more difficult to regulate. This was illustrated in May 2000, when the French authorities tried to bar Yahoo's auctions of Nazi items under broad French anti-hate speech laws, threatening the U.S.-based site with fines of as much as $13,000 per day unless it blocked French citizens' access to the items. Yahoo protested, saying it ran a French auction site which abides by local laws but could not effectively block people in France from going to other country-specific sites to access the objectionable material. In November 2000, a U.S. federal judge ruled that Yahoo was not bound to comply with French laws governing Internet content. Yahoo's case demonstrated how the true global nature of the Internet makes it particularly difficult to enforce different types of national regulation.

The Internet offers global access to information through web browsers, like Internet Explorer or Netscape. Web browsers are essentially a universal standardized technology. The standardization of web access makes e-commerce a viable option for all businesses, however small. It is difficult to overstate this last fact. Electronic trading is not a new invention: companies like General Electric and Hewlett Packard (HP) were trading electronically as early as the 1980s, using what was then known as Electronic Data Interchanges (or EDIs). But they first had to spend millions of dollars creating a unified interface for electronic interactions with their suppliers. Suppliers, too, had to incur large costs to install and use the software. Moreover, the HP software could be used only for trading with HP, and so on. This situation has changed dramatically. Nowadays, once a trading mechanism has been established on the web, the costs of participating are very small, because the enabling technology for e-commerce (browsers) is freely available to all.

The Internet brings together geographically dispersed buyers and sellers, significantly increasing the size of potential markets. For buyers, it provides easy access to catalogs and price lists of sellers. Most businesses on the Internet face relatively low entry, set-up and maintenance costs, although the costs of advertising and fulfillment are still high. Electronic retailers also face lower *menu costs* (the cost to the seller of changing its prices, e.g. print new menus, update price tags, etc.) compared with their "bricks-and-mortar" counterparts, which allows them to update their prices frequently in response to changes in demand or supply.

At present, Internet-based electronic commerce is, for the most part, restricted to online shops and services that are accessible via a web browser. A consumer can search for a product and purchase it by simply entering a valid credit card number. Such services are sometimes referred to as "first-generation" or user-driven e-commerce: the consumer uses the Internet to search and locate a specific product and to make a single purchase. These types of e-commerce application are now commonplace, and are likely to account for the bulk of electronic commerce for the immediate future.

But prototypical "second-generation" e-commerce applications are now beginning to emerge. Here the user—be it an individual or an organization—*delegates* the authority to transact business to a software program. E-commerce becomes automated.

The emergence of automated e-commerce

There are substantial cost savings from automating the business process. Using this technology, retailers can stay open, at no extra cost, for 24 hours a day, customers can search even when they are not logged on, and businesses can take better advantage of market opportunities by authorizing software programs to make decisions on their behalf. For example, consumers make use of "shopping bots" to search the Internet for the best deal of particular items, and businesses make use of automated "bidding elves" in complex online auctions.

Automated interactions are becoming increasingly important, partly because of "technology push"—the growth of standardized communication infrastructures and advances in automated negotiation technology—and partly because of "application pull"—such as web purchasing of goods, information and communication bandwidth, and the continuing industrial trend toward outsourcing. If anything can be termed "revolutionary" in e-commerce, then it must include these automated interactions between individuals and organizations.

Automated software programs increase the search power of users, and allow more extensive and "smarter" searches in large databases—a process, that is currently slow and may be off-putting to many users. These programs are also able to perform interactive searches on behalf of their users. For example, a ShopBot searching for airline tickets from virtual travel agencies on the web can match preferred dates, price range, class of travel and other features of the journey, without having to go back to the user, on whose authority it is operating, at any stage. If prices are negotiable, then it is possible (at least technologically possible) that programs equipped with some negotiation skills will do the bargaining on behalf of their users.

Similarly, this technology can be used by sellers to tailor the contents of their site. Most sites require that users register with them first. Of course, consumers benefit from being registered through a shorter process and faster and more efficient service. But it does mean that the seller knows the identity of the consumer surfing, and in particular details such as post codes, in real-time. An online catalog can be individually customized to match the user's likely requirements: all the seller needs to do is install the appropriate software—there are no further costs in rearranging the content. More generally, the company's site can be rearranged for the user. In particular, the technology can be used to offer different prices to different consumers. E-commerce provides the first real opportunity to practice this type of personalization and discrimination.

Much of the economic value of e-commerce arises from this kind of automation. The opportunities to use the Internet for business and comparison shopping are increased significantly by technologies that can take the place of activities previously done manually, especially those that were most costly in terms of data and working hours. And e-commerce, particularly automated e-commerce, creates new economic value, not only by making business processes easier but also by opening up new possibilities for market interactions.

WHY USE ECONOMICS TO ANALYZE E-COMMERCE?

Economics is a huge subject area. Traditionally, it is divided into microeconomics and macroeconomics. *Microeconomics* is the study of detailed individual decisions, while *macroeconomics* emphasizes the interactions in the economy as a whole, abstracting from the choices of specific individual and organizations.

There are many interesting micro- and macroeconomic issues arising from e-commerce. But this book focuses solely on the microeconomics and does not address such macroeconomic issues as electronic money and the effects of e-commerce on globalization. The main reason for this choice is that e-commerce is largely a business phenomenon—individual companies introducing new trading mechanisms and e-commerce applications. Although governments are looking to respond to these changes with appropriate legislation, the type of applications and strategies currently seen in the market are largely driven by market forces. This suggests that, before proper macroeconomic analysis can be carried out, it is necessary to understand the microeconomics of e-commerce.

As a science, economics is both descriptive and constructive. It can be used to *describe*—and therefore better understand— observed phenomena. For example, it can be used to describe why books are likely to be sold on the web, while other goods are not. Economics can also be used to *construct* economic institutions, such as e-commerce applications where buyers and sellers interact. For example, the theory of double auctions can be used to design an efficient web-based global market for steel. Both approaches are used in this book, the descriptive more in part I, which shows how to evaluate e-commerce applications, and the constructive more in part II, which explores how to design e-commerce applications.

Economics is a powerful tool for looking at the world, a means of analyzing how the economy, or a part of it, works and of making predictions about what will happen if something is changed. At its heart is a basic intuition of what incentives determine economic behavior: rationality, the assumption that people (and software programs operating on their behalf) act in their own best interests. Next, it involves a way of thinking about how economic interactions take place across the whole marketplace, something provided by game theory. And finally, it offers "solutions", some means of predicting and assessing the potential outcome or outcomes of all those interactions: this comes from the concept of equilibrium.

The useful assumption of rationality

The chief assumption underlying economic thinking is rationality, which can be broadly defined as the assumption that economic actors (be they individuals, organizations or even software programs) act in their self-interest (or, in the case of software programs, in the self-interest of their users). In other words, when presented with a number of choices, they—to the extent that they can—rationally choose the action that helps them best achieve their goals.

So, for example, companies will choose pricing strategies to maximize their profits, and consumers will look to pay as little as possible. If it is not known which action is the best, then it is assumed that economic actors will choose the action that they *expect* to be the best, given whatever limited information they have and their goals. [1] It is possible within this framework that people are altruistic or make choices that do not benefit themselves directly. As long as this is what they want—is part of their goal—there is no contradiction between the assumption of rationality and such behavior.

Is this assumption always justified? Of course not. Everyone is familiar with cases where people make choices that they later regret. But economics deals only with those cases where choices are "optimal". In other words, economics is all about explaining the interactions of rational agents. There are a number of justifications for this.

- First, there is no proper and robust theory of irrationality and it is therefore best to stick to what can be described.
- Second, in many cases in commerce, economic actors do try to act rationally (i.e. to make the best, or optimal, decision). Managers, for example, are paid to do what is best for the company they are running, and many consumers compare prices and other attributes of the goods and services they are buying. This argument goes further: even if people are unaware of their decision processes, over time, and especially in the cases where they care about the outcomes, they will behave *as if* they are maximizing some goals. These goals, whether they are aware of them or not, are what economists call *revealed preferences*—the real goals as revealed by actions.
- Finally, much of economics, and certainly much of what is discussed in this book, is to do with how individuals or organizations *should* behave. In other words, this book can be used by, say, managers to select what is optimal for their organization. Economics, the theory of rational choice, is the science that prescribes advice to organizations and individuals seeking to behave optimally. And if people

---

1 Suppose, for example, that the economic actor in question expects that action A will lead to a payoff of either $10 or $0 with equal probability, while action B is expected to yield payoffs of either $12 or $5. Then action B is preferred to A because its *expected* payoff is higher.

care enough about the outcomes (for example, if there are large sums of money involved), and if the rules are not too complicated, then they will try to behave pretty much as the theory predicts.

Using game theory to understand business interactions

It is common nowadays to think of the interactions between self-interested economic actors as *games* and of the actors themselves as *players*. Game theory, which has had a huge impact on microeconomics over the last three decades, is dominant throughout much of this book. The basic idea is that, just as the rules of most games like chess or poker can be described formally, so can the rules governing most economic interactions. And, just as players in a game play to win, so economic actors play to "win" their own goals.[2] So, for example, the seller of an antique chair and bidders participating in their web-based auction play a game where the seller's goal is to try and get the highest price and each bidder is attempting to win the object while paying as little as possible.

There are two significant points about game theory as a way of analyzing business situations.

- First, it provides a uniform language with which to describe the interactions of self-interested economic actors.
- Second, it defines the "solutions" or "equilibria" of games.

In analyzing games, economic actors are players and the actions and decisions available to them are referred to as their *strategies*. For example, each bidder in a sealed bid auction submits a single bid that must be a non-negative number, and so the set of positive real numbers are the bidders' possible strategies. Once all players have selected their strategies, the game is played and an outcome is realized.

For example, assume that the auctioneer of an antique chair gives it to the bidder with the highest bid and charges her this bid. Suppose now that there are three players, A, B and C, and

---

2 Paradoxically, game theory contributed very little to understanding of board games like chess—it turns out that chess is far too complicated to describe in terms of strategies—and yet managed to revolutionize the analysis and design of many economic institutions.

that A bids \$110, B bids \$70, and C bids \$95, then A will win the chair and will pay the auctioneer \$110. For a given selection of strategies, it is therefore possible to talk about the *payoffs* to each of the players. Continuing with the same example, it is clear that players B and C receive a payoff of zero. Suppose that A values the chair at \$150. Then A's payoff is \$150–\$110=\$40. Suppose further that the worth of the chair to the seller was \$55. Then the seller's payoff equals \$110–\$55=\$55.

So how do strategies and payoffs play out in the analysis of games? The main solution concept used by economists is the *Nash equilibrium*. [3] A Nash equilibrium is a combination of strategies, one for each player, which has the property that, given the choice of strategies of the other players, none of the players wants unilaterally to change their strategy. In other words, each of the players chooses their optimal strategy *given* the choices of the other players.

For example, consider the decision of firms concerning whether to adopt a new technology for electronic trading. Installing this technology is costly, but if at least half of the other firms in the market also adopt it, then the rewards outweigh the costs. This situation can be described as a game: each firm's set of strategies consists of two options: "adopt the new technology", and "do not adopt the new technology". It is easy to see that the strategy a given firm should choose depends on the choices made by the other firms: if at least half of the other firms adopt the new technology, then it is optimal to do so too. If fewer than half the other firms adopt the technology, then it is optimal not to do so.

What are the Nash equilibria of this game? Remember that in a Nash equilibrium none of the firms will want to change their choice of strategy. So, clearly, a situation where some of the firms adopt the technology and some do not cannot be an equilibrium. If the fraction of firms adopting the technology is greater than one-half, then each of the firms not adopting the technology would be better off changing their strategy. Similarly, if this fraction is smaller than one-half, then each of the adopters would have been better off not adopting the technology. So the only two "candidates" for equilibria are the cases where all firms choose the same strategy. And indeed, each of

---

[3] So named after the American mathematician John Nash, who formalized it in the 1950s. In 2002 the extraordinary life of John Nash became the subject of a successful Hollywood film, *A Beautiful Mind*.

these cases is a Nash equilibrium. If everyone adopted the technology, then no single firm would prefer to change its strategy. Similarly, no one wants to be the only adopter of the technology, because this is not cost effective.

This example demonstrates both the advantages and disadvantages of the notion of a Nash equilibrium. Clearly, the two outcomes are very different—all the players (firms) will be better off in the equilibrium where the technology is adopted. Yet both outcomes equally qualify as an equilibrium. So a Nash equilibrium does not reveal everything about optimality. But, since the outcome for each firm depends on the choices made by others, it is not possible to say something meaningful about the optimal choice of a given firm without reference to the choices made by others.

So a Nash equilibrium is a measure of stability rather than optimality. Recall the definition of a Nash equilibrium: "None of the players wants unilaterally to change their strategy." Think of economic situations as evolving: individuals and firms make choices and then update them in response to outcomes. Suppose that at some stage players arrive at a Nash equilibrium (for example, in this case, all firms, say, do not adopt the technology). Then they are likely to continue with whatever they are doing (at least for some time), because none of them can gain from changing their behavior. And so this situation is stable. But if they did not arrive at the Nash equilibrium (for example if only 80 percent of firms adopt the new technology), then at least one of them (e.g. any of the firms in the 20 percent that did not adopt it) does have an incentive to change. And so the situation is not stable.

The concept of equilibrium

The notion of equilibrium is central to modern economics. Economists trying to understand economic phenomena construct an analytical model and solve it by computing its equilibria. These equilibria are then thought of as the predictions of the model: since economic actors are assumed to be rational, they will continue to change their behavior as long as this is beneficial. Only in equilibrium does no one have an incentive to change, and so this is likely to resemble actual behavior, at least in the long run.

For example, in chapter 3 we study the implications for consumers and Internet retailers in adopting technologies, such as personalization and search agents. To do so, we first build a stylized model [4] of the interactions between buyers and sellers in electronic markets, where the technology investigated is not in use. We find the equilibrium of this model and compute the payoffs for buyers and sellers. Then we re-examine the same stylized model, this time allowing for the technology to be used, but keeping everything else fixed. This modified model will have a new equilibrium, and once we find it, we again compute the payoffs for everyone involved. Since everything in our analysis has remained fixed except the use of the technology investigated, we can say that the effect of using this technology say for retailers is described by the difference in their payoffs between the first and second equilibria. If retailers have a higher payoff in the second equilibrium, we say that they are better off using the technology; and so on. The equilibrium already takes into account the incentives and behaviors of all participants, and so describes the total effect of adopting the technology.

Similarly, economists carrying out a design assignment (for example, designing an auction for a government) use equilibria to try to predict the outcome of their mechanisms if and when they are implemented. While this is true in general, it is particularly true for e-commerce design, where participants can be shown what their equilibrium actions should be. Since these actions are in their best interest, they are likely to follow them. For example, the online auction giant, eBay, uses second-price auctions, where the equilibrium action for bidders is to bid their maximal willingness to pay. (Chapter 7 explains why this is the case.) On their site eBay state: "eBay always recommends bidding the absolute maximum that one is willing to pay for an item early in the auction. ... if one is outbid, one should be, at worst, ambivalent toward being outbid. After all, someone else was simply willing to pay more than you wanted to pay for it." And so the equilibrium outcome is not only a prediction of using the design: it can also be used as a prescription for participants, which in turn makes it a very likely prediction.

---

[4] A stylized model focuses on a few decision variables. For example, in one such stylized model firms compete only in prices, not in quantity or quality. In reality, most decisions involve many different considerations. It is normally difficult to model all these considerations, and so economists study stylized models, which allows them to focus on a small number of effects at a time.

This is the approach used throughout this book. Ideas are made precise by referring to formal economic analysis. The predictions of these models can be discussed by referring to their equilibria.

KEY ISSUES

- The value of e-commerce is best understood through a systematic overview of the economic development of e-commerce, thinking carefully through the incentives and interactions of buyers and sellers across the whole electronic marketplace.
- The Internet offers global access to information and a variety of trading mechanisms through a universal standardized technology: web browsers.
- E-commerce sellers face low *menu costs*.
- Much of the economic value of e-commerce arises from the automation (for example using agents) of interactions between consumer and sellers, and between businesses. Automated e-commerce creates new economic value not only by making business processes easier, but also by opening up new possibilities for market interactions.
- Economic theory can be used (1) to *describe* observed phenomena in e-commerce, and (2) to *construct* e-commerce applications.
- Rationality of individuals and firms is a useful working assumption.
- Game theory provides a useful language with which to describe interactions between economic actors. In particular, the notions of strategy, payoffs and Nash equilibrium are relevant.
- Equilibrium analysis is the central tool both in describing economic phenomena and in constructing economic institutions.

Chapter 3

E-commerce for Consumers

The Internet is emerging as one of the most efficient and popular channels for buying and selling goods and services such as books, computer hardware and software, music CDs, videos and airline tickets. More and more customers are discovering the advantages of shopping online and the range of products available for online purchase is expanding. Within only a few years, web-based retailers such as Amazon and Travelocity have emerged as major players in their industries. Established names in high street retailing, which initially snubbed the Internet, have now reversed their decisions.

This chapter provides an overview of consumer e-commerce, and considers the economic implications of Internet technologies for prices and product offerings, and for competition between firms. There are two key questions:

- What is the economic value added from buying and selling online—in other words, why trade online?
- Is it buyers or sellers who benefit most from consumer e-commerce?

THE IMPACT OF E-COMMERCE ON PRICES AND PRODUCT OFFERINGS

How is Internet shopping different from "real" shopping? There are two key differences.

- First, there is the ease of finding information and comparison shopping, especially for homogeneous products. This means reduced search costs compared with "real" shopping.
- Second, sellers can now have far more information about their customers, through "personalization tech-

nologies". These make it possible for retailers to know the identity of their consumers in "real-time", to access data on past shopping patterns, and to change prices and offerings where appropriate. In principle, this opens up the opportunity to engage in the following strategies: (1) product differentiation: offering different versions of the same basic product to different market segments; (2) price discrimination: charging different consumers different prices for the same product; (3) "push" marketing: tailoring marketing messages to individual customers; and (4) mass customization: low-cost tailoring of the same basic product for individual customers.

The advantages for consumers of shopping online

For consumers shopping online, it is easy to find what they are looking for, to match goods more precisely to their particular requirements and to compare prices. This is especially true for homogeneous goods like CDs, books and software, but also for more complex products, such as airline tickets and mortgages.

Suppose that you are looking to buy a music CD on the web. There are two ways to do this. You can either use any standard search engine, such as Yahoo or Altavista, type in what you want and get an enormous list of websites, then visit and interrogate each of them "manually" to find the price of the CD. This can be very time-consuming, and realistically, you will be able to check only a few of these sites. But it is still probably better than trawling round or telephoning stores, so there can be significant transaction cost savings from buying online.

A more efficient alternative is to employ a "ShopBot". Here you pick the category "music CD", type in the name, and let the ShopBot visit many sites,[1] interrogate them to find the price, and return with the lowest price (or an ordered list of prices, starting with the cheapest). If you were to shop for the CD in real shops, you would need to spend time visiting or calling the shops to find out the price. The time costs of getting

---

1 In theory, search agents can interrogate thousands of sites within seconds. In practice, only a small number of sites are actually searched. The reason for this is not technological, but economical, as explained later on in the chapter.

even three or four price quotes are considerably high. In effect, the ShopBot reduces these costs to zero.

There are many shopping bots currently available, such as DealTime, GreaterGood, (which promises to donate at least 5 percent of what you spend to the charity of your choice), Jango (now owned by Excite), mySimon, StreetPrices, StoreRunner and BidFind, which focuses on online auctions.

Although the basic idea is similar in all these companies, the actual technology is different. MySimon, for example, uses a search technology it calls Virtual Learning Agent, which mimics human shopping behavior. Evenbetter's bot pops up while any consumer who is registered with them is making purchases at sites such as Amazon, and displays a message indicating that the same item can be bought elsewhere more cheaply. With one click, the user is transferred to the site where the product is sold for less.

ShopBots are proving very popular with online shoppers. According to a study conducted in 2000 by the consultancy Angus Reid, 67 percent of 1,000 employees surveyed in the United States who have access to the web at work used ShopBots at some stage. This figure was exceeded only by the percentage of those accessing research or search engines and checking news and sports headlines. Comparison shopping was a more common reason to surf than checking the stock market, playing video games, using online banking services or viewing adult sites, the report says.

Although ShopBots tend to focus on homogeneous goods, where the only search dimension is price, there is no reason why the technology cannot be extended to deal with more complex goods. For example, Mortgagebot.com claims to have introduced the first website that enables consumers to comparison-shop among online mortgage lenders. The site compares rates and fees of the various lenders, searching for real-time price information and comparing the benefits of the lenders. The results are displayed in a format that makes it easy to compare different online lending options.

"Intelligent search agents will reduce the search time for consumers interested in online mortgages and ultimately provide borrowers with a lower cost mortgage," says Scott Happ, president and chief executive officer of M&I Mortgage Corp. and Mortgagebot.com. "By helping consumers discover which online lender has the best overall price, prospective borrowers can spend less time surfing and more time evaluating their alternatives." A typical search takes less than a minute. The company claims that conducting a similar search manually would take the average user about 30 minutes.

Interestingly, the site includes itself in the comparisons, although it claims to gather information from competing lenders in an equitable fashion. "Objectivity is critical. We intend to promote this tool as a consumer-centric web destination enabling borrowers to obtain quick, unbiased price information from the top online lenders," says Happ. But, as I explain later on in this chapter, there are good reasons for consumers to doubt such statements.

But retailers benefit too

Consumers undoubtedly benefit from shopping online. But there are also substantial benefits for retailers. For a start, sellers too can take advantage of reduced search costs to monitor each other's pricing behavior and may even be able to maintain *higher* prices.

But sellers also benefit from the second important difference between Internet and non-Internet shopping: the ability to know exactly who is surfing a site and to access their data in real-time. Personalization can be carried out according to website demographics (the user profile for a given site); individual domains (attributes inferred from the user's web browser); learning (by monitoring the behavior of users and learning their preferences), and correlation (by comparing the user's preferences with other users with similar interests and suggesting possible contents based on this correlation—for example, Barnes & Noble and Firefly have created a system that recommends books based on this method).

Using personalization technology, sellers can tailor their offerings to the requirements of the person surfing as deduced from their data. They can also personalize the price they are charging. The essence of personalization technology is the ability to measure the shopper's desire for the product and charge them accordingly and/or shape it to meet their precise needs.

Personalization technology in e-commerce takes place on several levels.

- First, sellers use a strategy of "first degree price discrimination", where different consumers are charged different prices for exactly the same goods based on their identity.

- Second, sellers use e-commerce to allow customization of goods and services at very low cost, sometimes at no cost at all—what Carl Shapiro and Hal Varian (1999) call "versioning".
- Third, the technology means that retailers can now know the identity of the users, and can handle previously risky transactions—such as arranging a test drive in an expensive car—without the worry that they are dealing with a fraudster, or a mischievous teenager.

E-commerce offers unprecedented opportunity to use consumer-specific information online. Because users normally register with sites (most companies either require registration or provide incentives for joining), the seller knows exactly who is surfing and can access their data in real-time. This allows sellers to tailor their offerings—and possibly the price they are charging—to the person surfing. The same data can be used to guess which goods or services the user will want next (for example, based on their past shopping pattern) and offer it to them in advance.

More specifically, in recent years an enormous amount of consumer-specific data has been collected by retailers and marketing companies (for example, through the use of loyalty cards and frequent flyer programs). Now companies like British Telecom (BT) and the UK's Post Office launch campaigns that offer firms the technology to target potential customers and tailor their marketing message to each individual. The same technology can then be used to develop customer profiles and relationships that are appropriate to each client individually. This is "one-to-one" or "push" marketing.

The data agency Experian has launched a software package that enables e-commerce sellers to recognize customers instantly. It can send the user's profile to retailers, including details of their wealth and the products they are most likely to buy. The site can then promote special deals to suit the user's tastes. It is widely expected that financial companies will use the program to offer cheaper insurance, better mortgage rates and tailor-made investments to customers.

Richard Fiddis of Experian told the *Sunday Times*:

> The potential is limitless. Customers will benefit from cheaper deals and special offers. You could find that you are offered a discount off your purchases if, say, you take out a special credit card with a cheap rate.

Companies will be able to target their products with extreme accuracy, so bespoke offers are a natural progression. It is no good advertising good deals on expensive cars to a 14-year-old child, and discounted computer games are of little interest to a chief executive. Such a scattergun approach will soon become a thing of the past.

Similar technologies are used in the United States: Shapiro and Varian (1999), for example, note that the online data provider Lexis-Nexis "sells to virtually every user at a different price".

Personalized pricing is likely to increase, because the technology that enables it is now in place. For example, in the United States the software company BroadVision offers a Retail Commerce Suite, which it says will allow any e-commerce player to practice "dynamic pricing": charging different customers different prices for identical products.

The pros and cons of personalized marketing

An Internet shopping study conducted by Ernst & Young found that, in general, the Internet is used for "considered" shopping. In other words, users who know exactly what they want are using the Internet to find the best deal. Of course, this happens too in the world of bricks-and-mortar shops, but much of the time consumers go shopping so that they can look around to see what is available. They do not decide in advance what they are going to buy. This poses limitations on what can be achieved by regular forms of advertising. Consumers who know what they want are less likely to be pay attention to advertising. Sellers can, however, counter this problem by using personalization technologies. The technology can be used not only to collect data on the user, but also to use such data to predict what users will want next and offer it to them in advance.

One technology that supports personalization is British Telecom's YOU CAN. BT, which dominates the UK telecommunications arena (with approximately 80 percent of the business market and 64 percent of the residential market), set up YOU CAN to "help companies transform their business functions and harness available technology in order to remodel the way they relate to their customers". The services include web-enabled call centers, news and information channels, and customized IP network services.

The idea is to attract and retain the custom of the most profitable clients. To attract new customers, sellers should target potential customers and tailor their marketing message to each individual. They can then go on to develop customer profiles and relationships that are appropriate to each client individually. YOU CAN's "customer relationship management" (CRM) services enable sellers to have a relationship with their customers and to learn what each customer wants and what they might want in the future. Sellers can then better respond to client needs and develop strong customer loyalty.

By developing databases that collect and analyze data on customers, companies can identify their best clients, i.e. those making them the most money, and concentrate their marketing efforts accordingly. CRM means that companies have the information to allow them to find the right products for customers rather than the traditional means of marketing, which involves finding the right customers for products. Marketing is thus based on relationships with customers rather than being conducted en masse. By storing information on previous sales and interactions, companies can develop one-to-one relationships with customers and build more long-term relationships with them.

YOU CAN offers a range of technologies to facilitate the attraction and retention of clients. Its electronic services play an important role. Electronic trading allows customers to order and pay for products over the Internet. Companies can also gather sales data in real-time, which enables them continually to monitor demand trends. The YOU CAN system collates information on every customer and then analyzes it to identify key groups and trends in behavior. Companies can use this information to tailor their marketing to the individual client and thus expand sales by offering them what they want, when they want it.

More generally, software is now available which monitors the behavior of users. "Spyware" is a general term describing software that monitors the behavior of the user, building and updating a database of personal preferences and habits. These data can then be used to second-guess what the user is likely to want to buy next. If, for example, the user has just bought a weekend trip to Paris, the software can recommend a travel guide. Or it might suggest a one-click reservation option for a restaurant near the theater they are going to visit tonight.

Naturally, not everyone is happy. Lawsuits have been launched in America against RealNetworks, DoubleClick and

Alexa, a subsidiary of Amazon. All allege that these data-monitoring companies infringe the individual's privacy. The toy maker Mattel outraged consumers when an American journalist discovered, after installing a Mattel game for his daughter, a hidden piece of software called Brodcast that was silently connecting his computer to Mattel's web server, which Mattel claimed was to check for software updates. But privacy protection lobbying groups around the world were quick to point out the software had many more capabilities, such as accessing any file on a computer, or tracking exactly how often Mattel games were played. Mattel quickly removed Brodcast from all its products.

The term "spyware" was coined by an American software writer, Steve Gibson, who has since discovered spying devices in hundreds of pieces of commonly used software. He believes that, if you regularly use a computer, you almost certainly have spyware on your machine. He claims that "there are about 23 million pieces of spyware currently installed on machines without the users' knowledge".

But the controversy over surveillance extends far beyond spyware. Almost every website uses a piece of code known as a "cookie" to track the movements of its users. These devices are no more than short text strings that pass from a given website to the user's computer, where they are stored. Cookies were designed to enable a website to recognize the user. When linked into an online retailer's profiling technology, the cookie compiles, for example, a record of all the holidays or cinema tickets bought by the user, building data incrementally into a profile reflecting the user's unique tastes and spending power. Such a consumer database is invaluable to the direct marketing industry.

The problem with both spyware and cookies is regulation. By its very nature, the web has no governing body and no police force to ensure that retailers care for and protect personal profiles in a responsible manner. Although the Data Protection Act in the UK ensures that consumers are made aware of how their personal data are to be exploited—and are given the option of having their confidentiality maintained—to enforce this policy across a medium as large as the Internet is impractical. The controversy over the future of personalization technologies was highlighted in 1999 in the furore that followed Intel's announcement that it would stamp a serial number onto each Pentium III chip, which allows websites to identify the computer being used to surf the net. Intel disabled the feature after privacy activists—with the support of the European Parliament—launched a boycott campaign. [2]

So what determines who wins?

It is clear that the value of consumer e-commerce technologies to both sellers and buyers is not as straightforward as it might at first seem. Consumers might benefit from being able to comparison-shop, but sellers too can take advantage of reduced search costs to monitor each other's pricing behavior. This is where economic analysis begins to offer valuable insights, since it suggests that sellers can use the technologies to maintain *higher* prices.

The increased ability of firms to treat their customers as individuals also has mixed effects. On the one hand, it allows sellers to charge their more loyal consumers higher prices. On the other hand, each consumer then becomes her own market, forcing sellers to compete more for their custom. The overall effect on prices and profits will depend on the specific features of the market, but economic analysis shows that in many cases consumers will actually be better off under individual pricing than under fixed pricing.

However, reaching these results demands some prior economic analysis of how markets operate and then thinking through the impact that e-commerce has on that operation.

In 1883, the French economist Joseph Bertrand made the observation that, if firms selling the same product compete only on price, they cannot make any positive profits. This result, known as the *Bertrand paradox,* can best be explained using game theory.

Suppose that there are two retailers competing in a market with total demand D. They both have the same unit costs, c—that is, identical staff costs, shop rents and advertising budgets. Consumers monitor the prices charged by the retailers and buy from the cheapest. A "strategy" for each seller is the price he charges for the goods. In game theory terms, a strategy profile is a pair of prices (p_1, p_2), where p_1 is the price charged by the first retailer and p_2 is the price charged by the second retailer. In this case, the *payoff* for the first retailer is $(p_1-c)*D$ if $p_1 < p_2$

---

[2] The original purpose of the chip's identification number was to support hardware digital certificates and other security measures that could be used to limit piracy by tracking users.

(that is, if it serves the whole market, and is making a profit of p_1-c for each consumer); 0 if $p_1>p_2$; and $(p_1-c)*D/2$ if $p_1 = p_2$ (that is, if the two retailers charge the same price and then split the demand between them).

What is the Nash equilibrium of this game? Recall from chapter 2 that any strategy profile where (at least) one of the players has an incentive unilaterally to change his strategy (in this case price) cannot be an equilibrium. Suppose that $p_1>p_2$ (that is, retailer 1 charges a higher price than retailer 2); then retailer 1 is making no profits. As long as $p_2> c$, retailer 1 can gain by setting a price in between p_2 and c. By doing so, he will gain the whole market demand (because his goods are now the cheapest) and make positive profits (because $(p1-c)*D$ is positive if $p_1>c$). This type of profitable price-cutting is possible as long as the cheapest price is greater than c. The Bertrand game therefore has a unique Nash equilibrium where both retailers set their prices equal to the unit cost, that is, $p_1=p_2=c$. But then neither retailer is making any profits: per unit sold the profit is zero, and so whatever size the demand, they both still make zero profits.

It is possible that retailers face different costs, for example if one sells CDs on the Internet while the other runs a music shop with high rents and staff costs. The Nash equilibrium of this game will be different from the previous case, although the logic is similar. Here the retailer with the lower unit cost can set her price slightly below the unit cost of her competitor, gaining the whole market demand and still making positive profits (because this price is still higher than her own unit cost). In equilibrium, the retailer with the higher cost will make no sales and no profits. The retailer with the cost advantage will serve the whole market.

Cost advantage may be the reason for the success of Internet retailers like Amazon, CDnow and Travelocity. But a closer look at the profits of the low-cost firm suggests that these profits diminish with the difference between their own costs and those of their second-cheapest competitor (because in order to gain the demand the retailer needs to set his own price below that of his competitor). The per-item profits are therefore equal to the differences in costs. If there is more than one Internet retailer, this difference is unlikely to be very large. The problematic aspects of the Bertrand result—that competing on price leads to no profits for anyone—are therefore relevant even if retailers have different unit costs.

The significance of the Bertrand result for competition in e-commerce

Bertrand's result is also known as the Bertrand paradox. This is because it shows how price competition leads to zero profits even if there are only two firms in the market. The same logic holds whether there are two or eight, or a million, retailers in the market: as long as the cheapest price is above unit cost, retailers can gain by price cutting, but this leads to prices equaling costs, and no profits. In reality, we tend to see that markets with a larger number of sellers are more competitive than markets with a small number of firms. It is rare that markets with two or three firms are at all competitive. Bertrand's result is a paradox because, although it is mathematically sound on the one hand, on the other hand is inconsistent with our view of reality.

Of course, several important features of real-world price competition are missing from Bertrand's analysis, and these can help explain the discrepancy between the game and what is observed in the real world. Taking into account the significance of these assumptions by extending Bertrand's analysis makes it possible to understand the realities of competition in e-commerce and whether it is buyers or sellers who are most likely to gain. Implicitly, the Bertrand model makes three assumptions.

- The first assumption is that consumers can effortlessly, and at no cost, find the cheapest price no matter how many sellers operate in the market—the issue of search costs.
- The second assumption is that sellers cannot react to price changes by their competitors; that is, the analysis assumes a "one-off" interaction—the issue of repeated interaction.
- And the third assumption is that products are completely identical and that price is the only factor in determining consumer behavior. Thus, the analysis excludes the possibility of brand loyalty, different levels of quality of service, product differentiation and mass customization.

The Bertrand result is a useful benchmark for the type of perfect competition that occurs if there is no friction in the market. The three assumptions can be thought of as the *sources* of friction, which prevent markets from being perfectly competitive. E-commerce is often dubbed "frictionless" (as in Bill Gates's term, "friction free capitalism"). Using economic analysis to examine the sources of friction in markets provides a better understanding of the economic value of the technologies that reduce friction. But this can only be done against the background of the Bertrand benchmark result.

CONSUMER RESEARCH AND COMPARISON SHOPPING: THE ECONOMICS OF SEARCH COSTS

If consumers need to invest less time and effort in finding information about the prices charged by various retailers—if search becomes less costly—then the competitive pressures on sellers are increased. At the same time, if search becomes less costly, then sellers are better informed and can therefore more easily monitor and react to their competitors' pricing decisions. So what does the economic analysis of search costs suggest will be the impact of the growing use of ShopBots, where search is indeed becoming less costly?

What can be learned from economic analysis

Bertrand's analysis assumes that consumers always buy from the seller with the cheapest price. But to do so they need to find this seller, and in reality the process of comparing prices can be lengthy and requires a certain amount of effort. Research shows that most consumers only "sample" prices, or do not compare prices at all. For example, many shops offer a "price guarantee" or "find the same product anywhere else for less and we will match this price". It turns out that this type of price guarantee is enough for many consumers: they buy without even checking the price of other sellers.

What is the implication of the fact that consumers (at least some consumers) do not compare prices because price search is costly? We can still get a single equilibrium price under the costly-search assumption. We now consider what this price will be (in other words, we begin by assuming a single price equilibrium and see what "candidates" there are for this price). Since all sellers charge the same prices, consumers have no incentive to do any search (because search is costly). All consumers will therefore buy from the first shop they visit. But if consumers never compare prices, then sellers have no incentive to lower prices! In fact, the only rational price to charge is the monopoly price—the price that maximizes their profits, given demand and *ignoring* other sellers—and certainly not the competitive price $p=c$ suggested by Bertrand.

Moreover, this conclusion is correct regardless of the actual costs of search. All that is needed for the argument to hold is that search costs be positive, even if such costs are very small and insignificant, as for example in the case of price comparison by telephone. Making local telephone calls is cheap in most places in the United States, and so the only cost of search is the time of spending a few minutes on the telephone.

This outcome is even more paradoxical than the Bertrand outcome. The "single price hypothesis" is therefore unlikely if search is costly. Instead, it is likely that retailers charge *different* prices and consequently that consumers (at least those consumers who care a lot about price, for example because they do not have much money) will compare prices before buying.

The theory of costly search when prices differ can be further developed. In fact, there are a number of important economic studies of consumer and retailer behavior when search is costly. One such study is by Hal Varian (1980), in which he suggests that consumers can be broadly divided into two groups.

- First, there are those who choose a shop at random and buy if the price is lower than a pre-decided reservation price (that is, the highest amount they are willing to pay for the goods or service, or the worth to them in monetary terms).
- Second, there are those consumers who first search for the cheapest price and then buy at that price.

Consider now the optimal pricing strategy of retailers in the presence of these two types of consumer. Each retailer will receive some share of the demand of the first type of consumer, regardless of its price, because these consumers do not compare prices. Retailers can occasionally conduct a sale, i.e. a price reduction on a number of their goods. If a retailer runs a sale, it has a chance of gaining the second type of consumer—those who search—at least if its price is at least as low as the other retailers conducting sales at the same time.

This scenario with two types of consumer can be described as a game. In the equilibrium of this game, retailers *will* occasionally conduct sales. The frequency of these sales will depend on a number of factors, such as the size of demand, the number of competing retailers and the proportion of informed consumers. In particular, the larger the proportion of consumers who search, the more frequent the sales. And this proportion is likely to increase when the cost of search goes down. So this analysis predicts that, as search costs decrease, the greater will be the frequency of sales, and consequently the lower (on average) prices will become.

Other approaches to the economic analysis of search (for example Burdett and Judd, 1983) focus on sequential search behavior: consumers get a price quote and, depending on this, decide whether to continue to search. At each stage, consumers evaluate the best price they already have against the chances of finding a better price if they continue to search. Clearly, the more expensive it is to search, the less likely they are to search for long. By considering the equilibrium of such analyses, it is possible to link consumers' search costs to price dispersion, i.e. the variation in prices charged by different retailers for the same product. While the approaches differ in exact details, they all have in common the fact that price dispersion decreases when search costs become lower. As search costs decrease, the market becomes more and more competitive and the prices come down toward their Bertrand level, $p = c$.

Economic analysis confirms that search costs can be a source of friction in markets, something that prevents them from being fully competitive. The higher the costs of search for consumers, the greater the opportunities for retailers to charge higher prices. On the other hand, as search costs become smaller, prices should decrease and approach unit costs. With the advent of consumer e-commerce in general and ShopBots in particular, the prediction of this analysis can finally be put to the test. ShopBots have the potential to reduce consumer search costs to zero. Does this mean that prices will drop dramatically?

Evidence of falling prices

The Internet offers consumers easy access to a huge range of information about prices, particularly of homogeneous goods where price is the dominant factor in buying decisions. In recent years, researchers have begun to gather data on prices of such goods on and off the web. These data can be analyzed to address the following questions: does competition on the Internet lead to lower and more comparable prices? Do Internet retailers adjust their prices more readily to changes in supply and demand? Are brand names and trust important for homogeneous goods sold on the Internet?

Research by Erik Brynjolfsson and Michael Smith (2000a) considers these issues in the context of the markets for books and CDs, both of which are homogeneous goods traded widely over the Internet. Their comparison of pricing behavior on the Internet and in conventional retail outlets suggests that prices on the Internet are 9–16 percent lower than those in conventional outlets. As more and more people gain access to the Internet, this suggests future difficulties for conventional retailers in terms of their being able compete on price if the substantial differences remain.

Jeffery Brown and Austan Goolsbee (2000) conducted similar research, focusing on the market for life assurance policies. Their results show that, for a given set of individual and policy characteristics, a 10 percent increase in the share of individuals in a group using the Internet reduces the average insurance price for the group by up to 5 percent. This is not the case for groups that were not covered by the comparison websites.

Brynjolfsson and Smith also find that Internet retailers' price adjustments are up to 100 times smaller than conventional retailers. The smallest price change on the Internet is $0.01, while for conventional retailers it is $0.35. This implies that lower "menu costs"—the direct costs to the seller of changing their prices (as in the cost of printing new menus for a restaurant)—for Internet retailers may allow them to adjust their prices more efficiently in response to changes in supply and demand.

In terms of price dispersion, there is evidence of substantial and systematic differences in prices across retailers. Prices on the Internet vary by an average of 33 percent for books and 25 percent for CDs, suggesting a great deal of dispersion despite the ease of consumer comparison. But when the prices are adjusted to take account of the market share of different online retailers, it seems that price dispersion is actually lower in Internet channels than in conventional ones. This reflects the dominance of certain heavily branded retailers such as Amazon and CDnow.

While price is an important determinant of customer choice, a second study by Brynjolfsson and Smith (2000b) indicates that, even among ShopBot consumers who can readily compare prices, branded retailers and those websites that consumers have visited before hold significant price advantages in head-to-head price comparisons. Such retailers have a significant advantage over their competitors in this setting. As an example, Amazon has a 5 percent margin advantage over unbranded retailers and a 6.8 percent margin advantage among repeat visitors. In other words, repeat visitors are willing to pay up to 6.8

percent more before they consider switching to another seller. Brynjolfsson and Smith conclude that consumers use brand as an indicator of a retailer's credibility, especially with regard to the aspects of a product that are difficult to specify in a contract, such as shipping time.

So economic research provides some support for the hypothesis that the Internet is a more efficient market in terms of price levels and menu costs. But the evidence of price dispersion suggests that retailer heterogeneity with respect to such factors as branding, awareness and trust remain important factors to understanding Internet markets.

Doubts about falling prices

Two points cast doubts on the argument that ShopBots will cause prices to fall.

- First, sellers can block their sites from being interrogated by ShopBots.
- Second, sellers can also use these shopping bots to regularly check each other's prices. This in turn can be used to maintain tacit price collusion, allowing sellers to charge high prices.

In most examples of ShopBot technology, not only can retailers block their sites from interrogation, but they actually have to register—and, in many cases, pay—to be searched. So why would a retailer pay to be forced into cut-throat price competition?

Indeed, it is worth considering the incentives of the ShopBot websites themselves, by asking how they make (or intend to make) profits. None of the companies charge consumers for using their services. Most of them charge sellers to be listed on their comparison shopping engine service, and many have arrangements with retailers to display their goods in a search. So the results given by the ShopBot are often biased toward retailers having agreements with the site.

Since participation is a *choice*, there are clear incentives for sellers to avoid direct price competition. In other words, by registering with a ShopBot site, the retailer is sending a signal to its competitors that it does *not* intend to cut prices.

Furthermore, since retailers too can find out what prices their rivals are charging, they can respond more effectively to each other's pricing strategy, and this may actually enable them to sustain *higher* prices. The intuition is that it will now be more difficult for sellers to secretly undercut one another so that every price cut could "trigger" a "punishment", for example by an all out price war. This threat can sometimes be sufficient to deter any seller from cutting prices.

Repeated interactions and trigger strategies

In Bertrand's analysis, retailers cannot react to each other's pricing strategy. What happens today is of no consequence tomorrow, for the simple reason that in this model there *is* no tomorrow (i.e., the Bertrand model is a "one shot" game). In reality, of course, most interactions between retailers are not limited to a single transaction. But if interactions between sellers are repeated, then this should form part of the analysis. So how can Bertrand be extended to deal with repeated interactions, and what implications does this have for consumer e-commerce?

Bertrand illustrates the incentives of retailers to undercut one another by charging a price that equals marginal cost. The analysis has a unique equilibrium where both sellers charge prices equal to marginal cost and make zero profits. But if sellers could somehow agree to charge higher prices, then they would all stand to make positive profits. For example, if sellers could agree to set their prices equal to the monopoly price, then they would split the demand between them and make high profits. (If there are only a few sellers, then these profits will indeed be substantial.) But in the Bertrand model, such an outcome, however desirable for sellers, cannot be reached. Even if sellers decide to collude, each one has an incentive to cheat by setting its price slightly below its opponent's price and winning the whole demand.

But what happens if sellers interact more than once? Perhaps they would choose not to undercut their opponent's price today because of the consequences of this on tomorrow's profits? It turns out that, even if these interactions are repeated a finite number of times, collusive behavior remains an unlikely outcome: in the final period, there will be no tomorrow to think of, and so the sellers' incentives are just as in the original Bertrand analysis. Consider now what would happen in the penultimate round. Sellers know that in the next (and final) stage everyone will charge a price equal to marginal cost, and so there are no incentives to collude today. Because whatever they do today will not be rewarded tomorrow, they may as well pick the rational one-off strategy, which is to set the price equal to marginal costs. Therefore rationality requires that, in the round before last, sellers charge prices equal to marginal cost and make zero profits. It is easy to see that the same reasoning implies $p=c$ in the round before the penultimate round, and continuing right back to the first round. So, even if the game is repeated a finite number of times, Bertrand's conclusion remains valid.

But if there is no final period, then this type of backward reasoning does not work. And in reality, there is no reason why there should be a known last period. Sellers could exist forever; at any rate, the date when they might cease to exist is unknown. It turns out that if the interactions are repeated infinitely—or even if they are repeated a finite number of times but the last period is not known in advance—then collusion is a possible outcome.

A pricing strategy in the infinitely repeated Bertrand model is an infinite list of prices (one for each period). These prices can depend on the prices set by other sellers in previous periods. For example: "Start by setting the price to the monopoly price, continue by setting your price at period t to the price set by your competitors in period $t-1$", and so on. Collusion pricing can be achieved using what is known as a *trigger strategy*: "Start by setting the collusive price and continue with it forever unless the other seller undercuts you. If they do, switch to $p=c$ forever". It is easy to see that if one of the sellers uses such a trigger strategy, then the others are better off cooperating throughout the repeated game. Moreover, through a more formal analysis (which is beyond the scope of this chapter) it is possible to show that trigger strategies are the best response to each other. That is, if your competitor is using a trigger strategy, then it is also your best strategy. So a situation where both firms are using trigger strategies to determine their prices is a Nash equilibrium of the infinitely repeated Bertrand model. And if both firms are using trigger strategies, the threat of punishment is sufficient to deter price competition—firms will continuously charge consumers the monopoly price.

If repeated interactions take place, therefore, it is possible for retailers to charge equilibrium prices above marginal costs. But to do so, they must be able to punish undercutting (if punishment is not possible, then the incentives to undercut remain), and to do that they need to monitor the pricing behavior of their competitors. ShopBots allow easy access to the current and updated prices of the competition, making secret undercutting more difficult and increasing the effectiveness of trigger strategies. ShopBots can therefore affect the prices of homogeneous goods in two opposing ways:

- ShopBots reduce search costs for consumers and consequently put pressure on sellers to reduce prices.
- ShopBots increase price transparency, which increases the incentives for retailers to use trigger strategies, resulting in higher prices.

Recently a number of economic models have been put forward, which seek to formalize these features of price dispersion in markets for homogeneous goods with ShopBots. Most notably, Michael Baye and John Morgan (2001) show that ShopBots[3] will—in the equilibrium of their model—charge firms high prices, resulting in partial participation. Another interesting model, by Ganesh Iyer and Amit Pazgal (2002) focuses on the pricing decisions of firms selling homogeneous goods using both ShopBots and other channels. Their model does well in explaining a large set of data on the pricing of books, CDs and videos using seven leading ShopBots and comparing with prices elsewhere.

INDIVIDUALLY TAILORED PRODUCTS AND PRICES: THE ECONOMICS OF PERSONALIZATION

Bertrand's approach to competition can also be extended to examine situations where sellers can differentiate their offerings. This framework, based on economic analysis first developed by Harold Hotelling (1929), can be used to examine the implications of personalization technologies. In particular, it makes it possible to understand first degree price discrimination—the ability of firms to charge individually tailored prices—and to explore the joint economic impact of individual pricing and mass customization.

Product differentiation

The Bertrand result is based on the assumption that the only attribute that matters to consumers is price. But, even for homogeneous goods such as CDs and books, retailers can create brand loyalty through advertising, quality of service and so on. Retailers who are successful in creating such loyalty are then able to raise their prices slightly above those of their

---

[3]   Or "Information Gatekeepers", as they call them.

unbranded competitor, in the expectation that not all customers will switch to the cheaper retailer.

In these circumstances, the logic behind the Bertrand result will not hold. If retailers manage to differentiate themselves, then it is possible that in equilibrium they are able to charge prices higher than unit costs, and consequently to make positive profits. How much profit exactly will depend on the degree of product differentiation. As a general rule, the more sellers differentiate their products, the higher their equilibrium profits. Hotelling's analysis extends Bertrand's by allowing firms to differentiate. It also provides a useful framework with which to study the effects of personalization technologies.

Hotelling's basic analysis works like this: two retailers, A and B, selling identical goods are located at either end of a line of length $L > 1$ (figure 3.1). L represents the degree of differentiation between the two sellers: the larger it is, the more differentiation there is (for example, through brand loyalty). Each consumer can be "located" along the line according to her degree of loyalty to the products sold by A and B. A consumer who is very loyal to A is located near to A, whereas a consumer who is not particularly loyal to either products is located in the middle of the line, that is, equidistant between the two retailers.

Figure 3.1: The Hotelling model

Once sellers fix their prices, consumers choose where to buy. Of course, sellers anticipate consumers' choices and will therefore set their prices so as to maximize their profits, given the expected response of consumers. Assuming prices are not too high (compared with consumers' willingness to pay), all consumers will buy from either A or B. Specifically, for any pair of prices pA and pB, there will be a point x': all consumers located to the left of that point will buy from A and all those located to the right of that point will buy from seller B. In economic terms, the consumer located at x' is indifferent as to the choice of buying from A or B.

Once point x' is calculated (as a function of pA and pB and of the distribution of the consumers and their degrees of loyalty to the two products), it is possible to calculate the profits of both retailers. And, given these strategies and payoffs, it possible to calculate the equilibrium prices.

There are two features of the Hotelling framework that are particularly relevant to the economic analysis of price discrimination and product differentiation.

- First, the equilibrium prices are always greater than c and hence both retailers make positive profits. Moreover, these profits increase as L, the degree of differentiation, increases.
- Second, the more loyal consumers are, the more profits firms make. More specifically, the equilibrium profits of both retailers increase the more biased the distribution of consumers is toward loyalty. In other words, as the degree of loyalty of the more loyal customers increases, sellers are able to charge higher prices and make higher profits.

Evidence of dynamic pricing

Retailers and marketing companies have been collecting an enormous amount of consumer-specific data in recent years. For example, loyalty cards and air mileage programs are used to collect data on the shopping patterns of individual consumers. And by employing data mining techniques, companies are able to infer from these massive databases the preferences of individual consumers. Even companies that do not (or cannot) collect data themselves can still purchase relevant consumer-specific information from direct mailing database specialists.

This consumer-specific information can, in principle, be used by sellers to undertake what is known as first degree price discrimination—offering consumers the product they want at a price they are likely to be willing to pay. Until now, however, such discrimination has been too costly—for example, a physical catalog that is individually tailored is hardly likely to be cost-effective.

With the advent of consumer e-commerce, this is no longer the case. In particular, personalization technologies significantly increase the ability of sellers to employ first degree price discrimination. For example, an online catalog can be individually customized by identifying the shopper and automatically redesigning the company's website to match the user's likely requirements.

In particular, the technology can be used to offer different prices to different consumers. Since online menu costs are practically zero, online retailers can change their prices to match what they expect the individual to be willing to pay for whatever they are selling. This practice of "dynamic pricing" has already been tried by the online book retailer Amazon. With its detailed records on the buying habits of 23 million consumers, Amazon is perfectly situated to employ dynamic pricing on a massive scale. But its trial of this strategy came under fire in September 2000 when the regulars discussing DVDs at the website DVDTalk.com noticed something odd.

The subsequent story was first reported in the *Washington Post* (Streitfeld, 2000). The newspaper describes the experience of one user who, after being quoted a price of $26.24, stripped his computer of the electronic tags that identified him to Amazon as a regular customer and was then quoted a price of $22.74 for the same DVD. As the news spread, another user wrote: "they must figure that with repeat Amazon customers they have 'won' them over and they can charge them slightly higher prices since they are loyal and 'don't mind and/or don't notice' that they are being charged 3–5 percent more for some items".

Amazon says the pricing variations, which stopped as soon as the complaints began coming in from DVDTalk members, were completely random. "It was done to determine consumer responses to different discount levels," said spokesman Bill Curry. "This was a pure and simple price test. This was not dynamic pricing. We don't do that and have no plans ever to do that." But an Amazon customer service representative called it exactly that in an e-mail message to a DVDTalk member. "I would first like to send along my most sincere apology for any confusion or frustration caused by our dynamic price test. Dynamic testing of a customer base is a common practice among both bricks-and-mortar and Internet companies."

The last statement is of course absolutely true. Physical stores sell the same products at different prices depending on, for example, location. Prices tend to be higher in the expensive neighborhoods. Car dealers negotiate with each customer the discount (and effectively the price) on a new car, the price of which is supposedly fixed. But while dynamic pricing, or price discrimination, is not unique to e-commerce, the possibilities to implement it on the Internet are much greater than in physical stores. As the *Washington Post* article says, "It's as if the corner drugstore could see you coming down the sidewalk, clutching your fevered brow, and then doubled the price of aspirin."

Personalization technology allows retailers to know the identity of their consumers in real-time, to access their shopping data, and to change their prices and offers accordingly. But, as Amazon found out, consumers' attitude to personalized pricing can be very negative. While Amazon spokesman Curry stressed that the price test lasted "only a few days", the *Washington Post* reports that Don Harter, an assistant professor at the University of Michigan, said he saw variable prices on Amazon at least a month before that.

Harter was conducting a study on the difference in DVD prices between an environment with variable pricing—such as the auction house eBay—and a presumably stable one, such as Amazon. "But my assumption of stable prices on Amazon was wrong," Harter said. Using two computers to check DVD prices—one through the University of Michigan using his Amazon account, one through Carnegie Mellon University with a computer that was unknown to the retailer—he found that items such as "The X-Files: The Complete Second Season" could vary by more than $10 in price.

Amazon's interest in dynamic pricing extends at least as far back as the spring of 2000, when it was discovered to be selling the Diamond Rio MP3 player, which it listed at $233.95, for $50 less to some customers. At this time, too, the complaints first surfaced on a message board, with contributors to the discussion mystified as to why some were getting better deals on the player than others. Amazon's explanation was the same: that this was a random test. It offered a refund to anyone who had paid full price.

Economic analysis of price discrimination

So is it in the interest of sellers to use personalization technologies to practice first degree price discrimination? At first sight this may seem an odd question, since the ability of a firm to employ dynamic pricing allows it to extract greater surplus from consumers, especially, as the Amazon example illustrates, from its more loyal consumers. This is what David Ulph and Nir Vulkan (2000a) call the *enhanced surplus extraction effect*.

But a key feature of the e-commerce environment in which retailers are now operating is that it is highly competitive. This introduces a second important consequence of any decision by sellers to use first degree price discrimination: it will intensify competition between sellers since they will now be competing consumer by consumer, what Ulph and Vulkan call the *intensified competition effect*.

In Hotelling's framework, retailers compete only for the indifferent consumer—all consumers located to the left of this consumer are "safe" for retailer A, and all the rest will go to B. With first degree price discrimination technology, this is no longer the case. Each consumer is now his own market, since retailers can set a price especially for him; and each consumer will decide where to purchase based on these price quotes. This will naturally lower sellers' profits, since it is perfectly possible that a consumer located to the left of a consumer who decides to buy from A may prefer to buy from B.

Generally speaking, treating consumers as individuals allows firms to charge more from consumers who are willing to pay more, either because they are more loyal to the brand or because they value the product or service more than others do. But it also forces firms into more competition, because each consumer is now a market to compete for. Ulph and Vulkan use the Hotelling framework to analyze the situation where sellers choose whether or not to use the new technologies to price-discriminate. The outcome depends on which effect dominates:

- the enhanced surplus extraction effect, which tends to increase profits; or
- the intensified competition effect, which tends to reduce profits.

As with Hotelling, in the Ulph–Vulkan analysis consumers are located along a line representing the degree of product differentiation. The two sellers are located at either end of the line. Sellers can either set a single price to all consumers, or offer each consumer an individually tailored price. If firms set individual prices, then the first observation is that, for the consumer located halfway between the two sellers, both sellers will offer a price equal to the marginal cost. (Essentially the Bertrand result holds for this consumer.) But the prices offered to the other consumers and the overall effect of profits depend crucially on how loyal consumers are to the brands of retailers A and B.

Broadly speaking, there are three cases, depending on the exact distribution of consumers' loyalty.

1. If most consumers are not extremely loyal to either brand, then the prices that a firm offers consumers will be almost everywhere lower than if neither firm discriminates. That is, the intensified competition effect strongly dominates the enhanced surplus extraction effect, and so firms are better off not using price discrimination and charging everyone the same price.
2. If some consumers are very loyal and some not, then a firm that price-discriminates will charge higher prices to those consumers located close to it than it would if neither firm discriminated. But since prices are lower for consumers in the middle, profits are still higher if neither firm discriminates. Overall, the intensified competition effect is still stronger.
3. Only if most consumers are extremely loyal to one of the two brands will sellers make more profits if they can price-discriminate than if not, because the enhanced surplus extraction effect becomes dominant.

The intuition behind this result is as follows. There are two effects at work—the intensification of competition between sellers, and the ability to discriminate. Consider first the impact of these two effects on prices. The first effect certainly lowers the prices to consumers who are least loyal to any firm—those in the middle. When there are almost no loyal consumers, the first effect means that prices are lower for all consumers. But when consumers close to a firm are extremely loyal, that firm can really discriminate. This offsets the competition effect and means that sellers can now charge higher prices to the customers that are closer to them.

Consider now the effect on profits. When prices are driven down for all consumers, as in case (1), then profits obviously fall when firms use first degree price discrimination. When sellers can effectively raise prices for their most loyal consumers, this may or may not be enough to offset the effects of low prices in the middle. Only when the ability to discriminate is very strong because of strong consumer loyalty (case 3 above) will discrimination actually be profitable.

In reality, it is likely that consumers' loyalty in the e-commerce environment is limited—recall the evidence that Amazon customers are willing to pay no more than 5–7 percent above prices from other online retailers. *So economic analysis suggests that allowing retailers to practice first degree price discrimination may in fact be good for consumers.* As long as markets are competitive, the most dominant effect of personalization technologies—which allow firms to charge individual prices—will be the extra-intense competition that they encourage.

What is more, e-commerce sellers have only limited opportunities to employ first degree price discrimination. For example, at present, consumers can hide their identity by logging in as new consumers (possibly from a different location), hence reducing the degree of price discrimination that firms can undertake. So if firms cannot gain from "perfect" price discrimination, they have even fewer incentives to charge individual prices when they can discriminate only partially. This strengthens the conclusions that allowing e-commerce sellers to use individual pricing may in fact be in the best interest of consumers.

The emergence of mass customization

First degree price discrimination, where different consumers are charged different prices for the exact same goods based on their identity, is only one way to discriminate between customers. In reality, e-commerce sellers use a number of pricing strategies in order to discriminate. In particular, technology makes it possible to customize goods and services at very low cost, sometimes at no cost at all.

"Zero gravity" goods, such as news and software, can be "mass customized" at no marginal cost once the appropriate software is installed. Online news providers like Reuters can offer any bundle of news and sell different bundles at different prices. Software retailers can offer the same packages in many "versions", which differ perhaps in only one or two features. By "versioning" products like news and software, retailers can more accurately price each version based on the profile of the typical consumer: the "top version", for example, is likely to be purchased by developers with greater willingness to pay, and so can be priced accordingly.

Even for goods like cars, e-commerce still allows the possibility of mass customization since it provides a useful means by which consumers can view the range of alternatives and prices on offer and communicate their choice. Take, for example, Customatix.com, a California-based sports apparel company that allows footwear fans to design their own sneakers, choosing their own colors, symbols and fabrics. The blueprint is transmitted to the company's factory in China, and the shoes are shipped within two weeks. With the help of the Internet, personalized goods can be made affordable for the masses.

Dell Computers was the first large company to use the Internet for mass customization of its products. Today, Levi's sells made-to-fit jeans for around $55; Nike sells customized sneakers for $50–$100 a pair; Mattel sells customized Barbie dolls for $40; Procter & Gamble will soon let coffee fans blend their own java; and at P&G-owned Reflect.com, cosmetics are made to order and shipped in packages labeled with the customer's name. Prices, typically, are not outlandishly higher than the ones on department store goods.

So how do firms engaged in e-commerce decide whether to follow a strategy of mass customization? A second research paper by David Ulph and Nir Vulkan (2000b) provides a framework for analyzing the incentives of firms to adopt strategies of both mass customization and first degree price discrimination. In particular, their analysis investigates the *interaction* between the two technologies, that is, how the adoption of one of these technologies increases the incentives to use the other.

The starting point for the Ulph–Vulkan analysis is that there are two separate and *independent* phenomena at work.

- *First degree price discrimination* arises when each unit of a product can be sold at a different price. In this framework, each consumer buys just one unit, so, by being able to distinguish between consumers, firms can effectively practice first degree price discrimination, offering the same product at different prices to different customers.
- *Mass customization* occurs where firms can offer a whole range of finely differentiated products at the same constant marginal costs without having to incur additional fixed costs on every differentiated brand they offer. Thus, firms can reap the benefits of customization without forgoing the benefits of scale economies: they have the opportunity to practice *second degree price discrimination*, where different brands of the same product are sold at different prices.

Because there are two independent processes at work, firms have a considerable degree of choice over their combined differentiation/customization and pricing strategies. So, on the one hand, a firm could choose not to customize and instead produce just a single product, but it could still choose whether or not to employ first degree price discrimination. On the other hand, if the firm chooses to customize, it has three possible pricing strategies.

1. It can engage in no price discrimination, and so sell all products at the same price irrespective of brand or consumer.
2. It could employ *second degree price discrimination*, selling different brands at different prices—though different consumers buying the same brand will pay the same price.
3. It could engage in *first degree price discrimination,* and so sell at prices that are in principle differentiated both by consumer and by brand. It is easy to see that in this case the firm will discriminate solely by consumer, since the firm wants to extract the maximum surplus from each consumer, and to do this it wants the consumer to choose the brand that comes closest to its taste. The firm does this by having prices independent of the brand.

Ulph and Vulkan's analysis explores the following questions.

- How does the degree of mass customization employed by firms affect their choice of price discrimination strategy?
- How does their price discrimination strategy affect their choice of customization?
- Which combination of the two strategies will firms choose?

Once again, they use the Hotelling framework to analyze price competition in differentiated goods between two firms. Consumers are located along a line of length L, representing the degree of product differentiation. The two firms are located at either end of the line. Firms can choose either not to mass-customize—in which case they just produce the single product at their end of the line—or to mass-customize—in which case they can produce at the same constant marginal costs a range of products over an interval from their end of the line. Firms can also choose what price discrimination technology (that is, first or second degree) to use.

Ulph and Vulkan's analysis produces the following results.

- The profits of the firm using first degree price discrimination technology are independent of the pricing strategy used by its competitors.
- A firm using first degree price discrimination technology is better off if it also mass-customizes, and this is true whatever the behavior of its competitors. By mass-customizing, it is able to extract extra surplus from its most loyal customers by producing for each of them exactly the goods they want to buy.
- The greater the degree of mass customization chosen by firms, the more likely they are to practice first degree price discrimination. More precisely, profits under both first and second degree price discrimination fall as the degree of customization increases. But they fall faster under second degree discrimination.
- There is an equilibrium at which firms practice mass customization and adopt first degree price discrimination technology.

A more detailed examination of the equilibrium reveals that firms would be better off not adopting either of the two technologies, but in the unique equilibrium firms will end up adopting both technologies and making lower profits. So the extra competition forced by personalization technologies is the dominant effect. This means that individual pricing and mass customization can in fact *lower* prices for consumers.

Ulph and Vulkan's (2000b) analysis of first and second degree price discrimination in e-commerce is complex. The incentives of sellers to use one technology will depend on (1) whether they use the other technology, and (2) the technology used by their competitors. Nevertheless, the conclusion that consumers' overall gain from the extra competition that sellers are driven into by adopting personalization technologies is robust and straightforward. These conclusions pose interesting questions for regulators and consumer groups alike, who seem to assume that personalization technologies, price discrimination and individual pricing are all bad for consumers.

Bundling

A further strategy available to e-commerce sellers is "bundling", that is, the selling of products and services in packages rather than as individual items. This practice is very common in the software industry: one of the core issues in the Microsoft trial was the legality of its strategy of bundling its Internet Explorer with the Windows operating system. This type of bundling occurs when sellers make it difficult (or in some cases impossible) for customers to purchase one of its products without purchasing another. This is particularly relevant to the software industry, because it is relatively easy to make software compatible or incompatible with other software or hardware. For example, many computer games will work only on certain playstations; word processors used not to be compatible with each other (at least in the days before Microsoft's Word was the dominant application); and so on. Readers who are interested in finding out more about the economic aspects of bundling—the incentives of sellers to bundle their products, and whether it should be allowed—are referred to the excellent discussion in Shapiro and Varian (1999).

But bundling can be used in other ways in e-commerce. One of the main difficulties faced by sellers is that the Internet is used for "considered", not "impulse", shopping. In other words, consumers know exactly what they want and use the Internet to find the best deal. This poses limitations on what can be achieved by regular means of advertising, because shoppers who know what they want and who value their time are less likely to be responsive to advertising.

This implies that sellers must find ways to provide online consumers with a unique shopping experience—one that is likely to make them buy more than simply what they were originally looking for—while differentiating themselves from their competitors. Bundling goods and services to create "value packs" can help achieve these goals. And indeed, virtual bundling is far easier than "real" bundling because there is no need actually to package the goods together and because it is easier to change the contents of packages in response to consumer demand.

This type of bundling is different from the type used by software companies, such as Microsoft. In fact, it can be carried out *between* organizations, resembling what marketers call *cross-promotion*. Cross-promotional marketing is the act of strategically aligning businesses that target the same market but do not directly compete with each other. In other words, a cross-promotion occurs whenever two or more organizations join forces to attract and/or serve their mutual market more effectively. For example, films directed at younger audiences now regularly run cross-promotions with fast-food chains.

Cross-promotional marketing is one of the least expensive, most efficient, least time-consuming and most credible methods for marketing a business. But it is also a relatively complex form of marketing.

- First, a retailer or manufacturer considering a cross-promotion strategy must find the right partner(s).
- Second, the right type of cross-promotion must be selected by the organizations wishing to team up.

These two process are interrelated and together amount to a considerable task, since there are various attributes that need to be considered—how good is the fit between the target customers? how good is the fit between the products? how good is the fit between the type of products and the type of cross-promotion selected?

A manufacturer or top brand retailer would also want to consider the medium- and long-term effects of the cross-promotion. For example, how will it affect its degree of product differentiation? A badly designed cross-promotion could, for example, increase sales temporarily but end up damaging the long-term exclusiveness of a brand name, causing more harm than good. On the other hand, teaming up with the right organization might actually increase the perceived desirability of a certain brand without actually costing anything to the participating retailer.

Physical limitation complicates matters further: customers want to see the goods they are buying, and organizations who employ cross-promotion are required to sort out shipping costs before any sale ever takes place.

These complexities may very well explain why cross-promotions are currently used either by large corporations, like Kellogg or Coca-Cola, or by physically close small businesses, such as shops in the same shopping mall. But the Internet opens new opportunities for cross-promotion and for cooperation between a huge number of organizations. The Internet can be leveraged to remove the geographical barriers inherent in cross-promotions of retail products. Online retailers can then offer their shoppers "package deals" with complementary products from other online retailers.

A number of start-ups are already working on providing retailers with the technology to use this type of bundling. For example Autonomy.com, which provides e-commerce solutions to retailers, offers its clients software for running cross-sales; others, like "Be Free", offer e-commerce retailers a network for joint advertising. It is likely that in the future "virtual" cross-promotions will become more and more common in consumer e-commerce.

CONSUMER E-COMMERCE IN PRACTICE: THE WALDO EXPERIMENT

Waldo is an experimental software program created by Andersen Consulting in 1996 and written up by Bruce Krulwich (1997). Described as a "lifestyle finder", it can interact with its users to collect data on their likes and dislikes and then generate a general profile of them. These profiles can be used for a number of purposes, such as recommending music or websites that the user might find interesting.

The generation of user profiles is becoming more common and a sample of the user's interests and characteristics are generally used to form them. The profile, once developed, can be used in a number of ways to carry out personalized tasks on behalf of the user. One common application process uses input data on the user's taste in music or movies: by learning about the user's actual likes and dislikes, the profile generated can go on to recommend further albums or movies.

Programs like Waldo take a new approach to user profiling, known as *demographic generalization*. The user profile is generated according to demographic data from a database containing the interests of people across a whole country, in this case the United States. The questions answered by users about their interests are used to classify them in terms of the demographic data. Generalizations can then be made about the user from these classifications.

The demographic system that Waldo uses, Prizm, divides the population into 62 demographic "clusters" according to their purchasing history, lifestyle characteristics and other survey responses. The system is based on a survey of 40,000 people, census data, catalog purchases and similar information sources. The database has information on 600 variables referring to either a specific lifestyle characteristic, activity or purchase. Examples of the variables include whether the person owns a dog, buys champagne regularly or watches the news every night. Each cluster is assigned a mean and standard deviation for each variable, which indicates the likelihood that people in that cluster have that characteristic.

For a given set of input data, the program finds the set of clusters to which the user is most likely to belong. If there is only one cluster that matches, then the data on that cluster can be used to create a complete profile for the user. But if more than one cluster is a possible match to the user's data, the demographic variables that are similar across all the matching clusters are used to form a partial profile of the user. Alternatively, if there is a large number of matching clusters, the program may identify the variable that best differentiates the possible clusters to which the user belongs and prompt the user for further information. It is always possible therefore for the program to form at least a partial profile of the user. An important point is that this can be done through minimal interaction with the user.

The program can use the clusters to create a user profile that is much broader than just the areas on which the user has given information. The profile created covers a much wider range of areas than those for which the user has been questioned, since information about the user can be inferred by matching with appropriate clusters.

For example, consider a user who gives the following information: watches CNN, plays squash and reads novels. Given this information, several clusters might be found that match the user. The people belonging to these clusters enjoy such activities to a greater extent than average, and so the user is more likely to belong to one of these clusters than to any other. From here, the program can create a partial profile of the user or go on to refine its information on the user and form a complete profile.

Waldo the Web Wizard

In order to make the software program more appealing to web users and entice them to participate in the experiment, the creators called it Waldo the Web Wizard. Waldo is a fortune-teller who interacts with his users through the use of cartoon pictures and amusing prose. Participation in the experiment was good, and data were collected on over 20,000 users.

Waldo asks users eight questions, each of which has five or six possible answers. The topics on which users are questioned are:

- the type of newspaper or magazine they read;
- the type of TV programs they watch;
- the last vacation they had;
- their free-time activities;

- the music they like;
- the type of car they own;
- the type of drink they like;
- the style of home they live in.

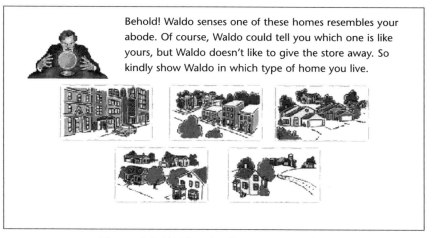

Behold! Waldo senses one of these homes resembles your abode. Of course, Waldo could tell you which one is like yours, but Waldo doesn't like to give the store away. So kindly show Waldo in which type of home you live.

Figure 3.2: Waldo asks the user a question

Figure 3.2 illustrates the process for the last of these questions. In this case, the user then selects the image that best matches their house.

Once Waldo has created a user profile, he recommends websites in which the user might be interested. Three types of recommendation are made, with five links given for each category:

- things the user could buy;
- places the user could go;
- stores the user could shop at.

As an example, consider someone who plays tennis, watches the Home Box Office cable channel and reads the business section of the newspaper. Through the responses to his questions, Waldo would discover that this person likes sports, business news and watching movies. There are several clusters in the dataset that match such a user. Waldo would thus ask a further question to try to narrow down the matches and so create a more accurate profile. He would ask the user what kind of neighborhood he lives in. If the user responds that he lives in a

From your answers, Waldo sees you in younger days listening to "In-A-Gadda-Da-Vida" in a haze of incense. Or perhaps it was "Stayin' Alive" in a frenzy of platform shoes and strobe lights.

Now it's the music of Barney and Disney's mouse that fill your home. You love to exercise and to travel. You're health conscious. You feel the best you've ever felt. And yet Waldo sees more …

○ Sounds right ○ Somewhat ○ A bit ○ Nope

Things you can buy

○ Y ○ N CD Link – this web site offers truespeech audio for most new albums, and some .WAV samples of every track on a CD.

○ Y ○ N Wall Street Journal Online: provides information regarding the Wall Street Journal, including how to subscribe to the online edition.

○ Y ○ N Mover Sportswear – live by aspiration, not expectation. This web site contains information on Mover products, a catalog and ski tips.

○ Y ○ N Webfoot Car Lot – Acura information: everything you ever wanted to know about Acuras.

○ Y ○ N Homelite Chainsaws – detailed information about Homelite chainsaws, with pricing info.

Places you can go

○ Y ○ N Sara's City Workout: give the Internet a workout – find out about the latest aerobics seminars and conventions from Sara.

Figure 3.3: Waldo's output

small city, Waldo can conclude that he is most likely to belong to the cluster named "upwardly mobile". This group is characterized by young white-collar families. People in this cluster tend to read science and technology magazines, listen to progressive rock music and use financial planning services.

Figure 3.3 shows Waldo's output. The output shows a cartoon of the type of user along with a short lifestyle description. It then has recommendations of links the user might like to visit.

Experimental results and possible applications of Waldo

Waldo was launched on the web on the August 26, 1996. It was used over 20,000 times. Of these users, almost 7,000 submitted opinions on the recommendations made. The conclusions from the experiment were that the generalization approach to user profiling appears to make effective use of a small amount of user information to create a user profile by leveraging a large demographic system. But the ability to operate from a small amount of input information comes at the expense of the accuracy of the recommendations the system is able to achieve. Only 24 percent of users found that Waldo accurately described their lifestyles, while 23 percent reported that the description was nothing like them at all. Overall, however, 60 percent of users found that Waldo's description at least partially described their lifestyles.

One application of this type of profiling is online advertising. Profiling could greatly improve the targeting of online information sent out to web users. Currently, most online advertising is targeted in a random fashion. Using technology like Waldo could enable such advertising to be much more accurate without needing personal information about the users.

Lessons from Waldo

The Waldo experiment illustrates both the strengths and the weaknesses of personalization technologies.

- Large databases can be used to create useful classifications of consumers—consumer profiles—that can be highly predictive of preferences and future behavior.
- The process of learning about the user can then be reduced to matching them to one or more of these consumer groups. Using a small set of observed choices made by the consumer, a relatively good match can be found.
- However, the process is not very accurate. The list of questions may be too general and too small.
- Instead, personalization can be carried out by an application residing on the user's browser. The user can install such an application when the latest versions of Netscape or Internet Explorer are being set-up. The application will be able to update the information given by the user at the set up stage and to narrow its user's profile. Since (as the analysis of this chapter shows) personalization can be good for consumers, over time, consumers are more likely to see the benefits from using such applications.

KEY ISSUES IN CONSUMER E-COMMERCE
Consumers

- ShopBots do not always return with the best price. Check the small print to see if the site maintains a "preferred merchandise" agreement with one of the sellers. As a rule of thumb, look for another price quote elsewhere.

- Personalization can be good for you. Use the fact that you can shop elsewhere to elicit good prices.

Retailers

- Allowing consumers to compare prices may be a profitable strategy. Especially if you have a long-term relationship with your competitors, you can all benefit from allowing consumers to compare prices.
- Personalization technology is not always good for business. It can increase competition and reduce profits.
- Personalization can be used to encourage your consumers to buy more, by using individually tailored push marketing, and giving them a unique shopping experience online.

Regulators

- Consumers' interests are best served through ensuring that there is sufficient competition. Banning personalization—or the infrastructure technology that enables it (like the Pentium III processor)—can actually harm competition.

Chapter 4

Business-to-business E-commerce

Business-to-business (B2B) e-commerce describes the interactions between firms that take place electronically via digital media. In particular, the term is used to describe electronic exchanges, web-based auctions and various other applications that automate the interactions of firms with their suppliers and corporate clients. Although consumer e-commerce has tended to get most of the media coverage, interactions between firms account for the vast majority of e-commerce transactions—over 90 percent, according to most estimates.

This chapter provides an overview of business-to-business e-commerce, focusing in particular on the economic advantages of trading through e-commerce and comparing the advantages and disadvantages of the three main forms of electronic market. In broad terms, firms can trade online via "one-to-one" or direct negotiations; by participating in "one-to-many" auctions; or through "many-to-many" exchanges, where there are many potential buyers and sellers at any given time. There are two key questions:

1. What is the economic value added in trading with other businesses online?
2. What is the preferable and most profitable online trading mechanism?

TYPES OF B2B E-COMMERCE

More and more companies are using the Internet to trade goods and services with their clients and suppliers. The obvious advantage of the Internet is that anyone anywhere in the world can access an electronic market at any time. All that is needed is access to a web browser. So setting up a marketplace on the Internet offers potentially unlimited participation at low cost. With the increase in wireless access to the Internet (for example, using WAP technology), the opportunities for web-based markets increase dramatically. For example, truck drivers can access the web from their cellphones to pick up loads on journeys when they happen to have free space.

Internet-based markets facilitate reliable and liquid trade of goods, because they can bring together geographically dispersed buyers and sellers, allowing them to transact in real-time or over different time zones, thus increasing the potential size of the market significantly. The growth of e-commerce is supported further by growing standardization of communication infrastructures over which different organizations can interact and safely carry out transactions (for example Netscape's Collabra software, which allows rich information specification and negotiation possibilities).

There are a number of basic economic propositions underlying business-to-business e-commerce applications: content aggregators, auctions, exchanges and B2B specialists. Content aggregators connect buyers and sellers through direct negotiations, which are the subject of chapter 6. Online auctions are explored in more detail in chapter 7, while exchanges (many-to-many markets) feature in chapter 8. B2B specialists use all three types of interaction.

Content aggregators

Content aggregators help buyers in fragmented markets to select products by providing up-to-the minute price and product information and a single contact point for service. Unlike exchanges—which bring together buyers and sellers of essentially the same product—content aggregators focus on bringing together buyers and sellers who are in the same industry but trade in a variety of products or services. A good example is Chemdex, which provides a one-stop shop for academic researchers and companies in the pharmaceuticals and biotechnology business to purchase all their supplies.

Chemdex claims to be the world's largest source of biological chemicals and reagents, with more than 170 suppliers and a vast electronic catalog listing more than 460,000 laboratory products. Before the emergence of the Internet, this market was inefficient and fragmented. Scientists were using dozens of catalogs, which were frequently out of date, and were making many telephone calls. Life-science companies, under increasing competitive pressure, were looking for ways of speeding up R&D processes and reducing their costs. Suppliers were hampered by the logistical inefficiencies inherent in the distribution of paper catalogs.

Chemdex's founders created a single, efficient marketplace on the Internet for all three of the communities it serves. For researchers it has created chemdex.com, a web-based catalog with powerful search engines and all the information required to make a purchasing decision. For business clients Chemdex has developed its own procurement and integration software to complement its website.

Auctions

Auctioneers offer a channel for sellers to dispose of perishable or surplus goods and services at the best possible prices, and for buyers to get bargain prices. Prominent online examples are eBay and uBid. Other, more specialized auction sites are used by members only, for example the Converge exchange auction facility used by companies like Hewlett–Packard and Compaq.

The vast majority of auction websites sell goods and services via English auctions, the arrangement in which the price rises continuously until there is only one bidder left willing to pay it. But other auction types are also used, including Dutch auctions, where the price drops until some bidder accepts it; sealed bid auctions, where bidders submit an offer unaware of what other bidders are offering; and reverse auctions, where it is the buyer who is the auctioneer and the price drops until there is only one seller left bidding.

Exchanges

An exchange brings together many potential buyers and sellers, creating liquidity in otherwise fragmented markets, lowering average stock levels by matching bid/ask offers, and acting as a neutral third party, enforcing market rules and settlement terms. Stock markets are the classic examples of such exchanges. In the past, these offered a physical marketplace for trading securities, but more recently they have migrated to electronic networks of buyers and sellers. Markets for communication bandwidth, such as RateXchange and Band-X, are good examples of exchanges that exist only in online form.

Bandwidth exchanges came into being because, while telecommunications infrastructure now spans the world, no single company connects with every part of it. As a result, telecoms companies and Internet service providers (ISPs) are obliged to transmit data on networks they do not own. This involves negotiating the right to use bandwidth on these networks. For telecoms companies, such negotiations are traditionally time-consuming and involve contracts for access to large amounts of bandwidth to last several months or years. For ISPs, negotiations over rights to transmit specific amounts of data over a given network are made even more difficult by the inability to monitor the source of packets flowing onto a given network. Instead, ISPs negotiate interconnection agreements with each other, where they can freely transmit and receive from each other's network. Larger networks (particularly those providing parts of the high speed Internet backbone) are willing to connect to smaller networks only on receipt of a negotiated payment.

But recent advances are altering the nature of this business. New technologies, such as the HP SmartInternet system, offer accurate monitoring of Internet traffic, which makes it possible for networks to cross-charge each other based on actual usage rather than estimates. The Web also allows negotiations between various communications companies to take place more rapidly and transparently. Companies like RateXChange and Band-X provide meeting places where companies can (anonymously) post requests to buy or sell bandwidth. Band-X Switched offers a marketplace where companies can actively negotiate with each other over prices, and deliver the agreed capacity by connecting to a switch belonging to Band-X.

Band-X are moving bandwidth trading from a slow, time-consuming business that results in long-lasting contracts to a more lightweight business process, potentially resulting in shorter duration contracts. In the future, every single phone call or even every single IP packet might result in new negotiations with various providers to determine the cheapest route it should take to its destination.

B2B specialists

Business-to-business specialists are concerned less with specific goods and services and more with the *process* of setting up electronic markets. These firms develop a variety of online trading mechanisms, often teaming up with an industry specialist as in the case of Exostar and the aerospace industry, the example of B2B e-commerce in practice discussed in detail at the end of this chapter. The incentives for firms within an industry to turn to the skills and experience of a B2B specialist to create an Internet-based market are strong: as Figure 4.1 illustrates, the costs can be very high.

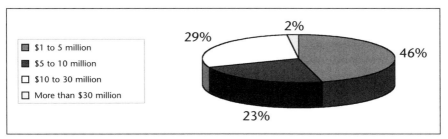

■ $1 to 5 million
■ $5 to 10 million
☐ $10 to 30 million
☐ More than $30 million

2%
29%
46%
23%

Figure 4.1: The range of costs of setting up an electronic market, based on a survey of a 100 Net marketplace executives
Based on: Jupiter Communications, September 2000

Examples of B2B specialists include Ariba, CommerceOne, VerticalNets and FreeMarkets. Ariba, for example, offers companies a flexible platform that allows them to access all possible customers, suppliers and markets over the Internet. The foundation of the platform is its open B2B network, which allows businesses of any kind, anywhere in the world, to connect, communicate and trade. Ariba's declared goal is "to help companies to get their applications to work together and to share information and resources with their trading partners". The result—it is hoped—is potentially more efficient B2B transactions, since businesses will be better informed and will have access to much broader markets.

However, after the fall in share prices (which saw all of the companies listed above losing more than 90 percent of their market share), these companies now distance themselves from the e-marketplace model. For example, CommerceOne, which once styled itself the "e-marketplace company", now prefers to be known as the "business internet company". Ariba now says it provides "enterprise spend management" solutions. VerticalNet recently announced that it would sell off its network of 59 e-marketplaces and instead focus on selling software.

WHY TRADE ONLINE?

Automating trade between firms makes sense. Much of this trade is stable, with companies trading with the same suppliers again and again. In most medium to large organizations, a number of people are involved in the purchasing process. They will typically have a purchasing strategy, identifying what they want—raw materials, office supplies, etc.—and how they rank the attributes of these various inputs, such as price, product quality and quality of service. Such a process lends itself to automation: a computerized system can be fed these data so that it can carry out automatic searches and possibly even determine automatically from whom to buy.

Long before the Internet became a popular medium for doing business, there were attempts to automate the interactions between large organizations and their suppliers. These systems generally consisted of trade-facilitating proprietary software forced on suppliers by a single large buyer. For example, Hewlett–Packard produced software for use by all its main suppliers, but these systems were very expensive to implement. Suppliers of Hewlett–Packard would have to spend large sums of money to implement a system that worked only with one client. Consequently, these systems were used only by large organizations, and then only for large transactions.

With the emergence of the web, and in particular of web browsers, which provide a uniform and cheap access to any company's site, the cost of setting up automated trading and electronic markets fell considerably, and the phenomenal growth of B2B e-commerce soon followed.

Clearly, there are many advantages from automating the purchasing process, notably:

- increased efficiency;
- cost savings;
- better control.

First and foremost, business e-commerce increases efficiency. Most electronic procurement systems are capable of automatic searches, comparing attributes like price and quantity. Moreover, they do so with far greater efficiency then any human. Indeed, it is useful to think of business e-commerce as a natural extension of the automation process that started in the 1970s. First, databases and back-office operations were automated, then came front-office, and now it is the turn of the interactions between organizations.

Second, and along the same lines, there are substantial cost savings from employing such systems. They are significantly cheaper than using human employees to do the same task:

while e-procurement systems are expensive to set up, once they are in place their running costs are very low, so over time their cost saving increases. The automation of the purchase-to-order process results in considerable savings over time, freeing an organization's human resources to focus on whatever they can do best. There is already considerable evidence to support the claim that Internet-based procurement automation dramatically improves the purchase-to-order process.

Finally, e-procurement systems not only reduce the cost of purchasing, but also allow an organization to take better control over its spending strategy. Many firms continue to buy at the same price from the same suppliers because it is too costly and difficult to be constantly searching for new ones and/or renegotiating existing agreements. But this has one great disadvantage: every time the approved suppliers cannot match current needs, organizations end up buying "off-contract", losing out on volume discounts, pre-negotiation agreements and so on. Such off-contract purchases—known as "maverick" or "rogue" purchasing—are estimated to add up to 40 percent of annual spending by U.S. firms on procurement. By automating the procurement process, firms should be able to reduce this figure considerably.

Figure 4.2 cites the reasons to use e-commerce for procurement given by 50 purchasing executives of large firms.

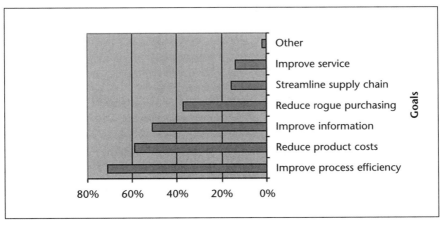

Figure 4.2: Reasons to procure electronically, based on a survey of
50 purchasing executives at companies with sales of $1 billion or more
Based on: Forrester Research, August 2000

HOW FIRMS CHOOSE THE MOST PROFITABLE WAY TO TRADE

A key feature of business-to-business e-commerce is the variety of trading mechanisms available for most goods and services: direct negotiations, auctions and exchanges. For example, many firms can now purchase raw materials such as metal, cement and steel via a web-based market, at a number of auction websites or by directly negotiating with various suppliers. So the key question is how firms choose between different trading mechanisms. In the rest of this chapter we ask what influences the choice by a single seller (or a single buyer) of whether to use an auction or direct negotiations? What are the incentives for all sellers and all buyers to participate in electronic exchanges? And is it better to trade through an auction or an exchange?

But before exploring the incentives to choose particular trading mechanisms, it is important to understand what motivates firms to trade in the first place. This is where economic analysis begins to offer useful insights.

The value from trading can be divided into two components: the likelihood of finding someone to trade with, and the gains from trade once a trade partner has been found. These two components can sometimes be in conflict. For example, in an auction the seller will probably find a buyer, but the price is somewhat out of the seller's control. In contrast, placing an advertisement in the classified advertisements section of the newspaper does not in any way guarantee finding a buyer, but when someone does call, the seller has a great deal of control over the final price.

Different methods of trading offer different degrees of "efficiency"—the gains for the potential participants' net of their costs of trading. At one extreme, bilateral or "one-to-one" bargaining can be very inefficient, as is explained below. At the other extreme, exchanges—markets involving many buyers and sellers—can be very efficient.

In terms of *overall* efficiency, exchanges tend to be better than bilateral trading mechanisms. But of course, no individual firm cares about the overall efficiency of the market; instead, each is concerned with its own profits. It is perfectly reasonable that some firms will prefer to trade via an inefficient mechanism, precisely because this inefficiency works to their advantage. So the question is: if firms are given the choice between trading mechanisms, which one will they choose?

The answer to this question is complicated, because which trading mechanism is best for a given firm will depend on the choices made by other firms. For example, there is little point in being the only firm in a trading mechanism or in conducting a reverse auction for raw materials if there is to be only one bidder. Addressing this question demands more precise definitions of what is meant by trading mechanisms and efficiency. In the rest of this chapter we will see that:

- auctions should be preferred to direct negotiations as long as the number of bidders in the auction is larger than the number of parties to negotiate;
- electronic markets will be preferred to direct negotiations (for example with suppliers) by traders with a "weak" bargaining position;
- the affect of these "weak" traders switching to markets will, in the long run, be that all trade will take place through markets.

Trading mechanisms and efficiency

In formal terms, a trading mechanism is a set of rules (or contracts) that govern the interactions between organizations and individuals. It is also a coordination device, bringing together buyers and sellers of goods and services in order to facilitate trade. Examples include the classified advertisements sections of newspapers, car dealerships, financial markets, department stores, web auctions and electronic exchanges like Exostar, described at the end of this chapter.

Trade is possible when two (or more) parties can mutually benefit from exchanging goods or services, normally in return for money. For example, if a certain product is owned by person A, and if person B is willing to pay a higher price for it than the price A requires for parting from it, then trade is possible between A and B. If trade is actually to happen, B needs to know that A owns the product and that she is willing to sell it; and A and B need to find each other and agree a price at which the transfer will take place. Trading mechanisms facilitate the trade by bringing A and B together and setting up the rules by which they can agree the terms of the trade.

More formally, the difference between the buyer's willingness to pay and the seller's minimal acceptable price is called the *surplus*. For example, if the buyer is willing to pay any price up to $50 for a second-hand book and the seller is willing to accept any price above $20, the surplus is $30. If they agree a price of $25, then the buyer's share of the surplus is $25, while the seller's share is only $5.

In some trading mechanisms, like classified advertisements, the purpose is only to bring buyers and sellers together, for example by informing buyers what sellers have to offer. Buyers and sellers are then left to negotiate the terms of the deal. In other cases, such as financial markets, the rules of the trade are quite strictly defined, so that there is no bargaining whatsoever between potential buyers and sellers. Such rules are efficient if negotiations are frequently repeated, because they reduce the time and effort it takes for the parties to negotiate directly with each other.

The rules used by the trading mechanism will affect the behavior of the participants and, consequently, the outcomes. A properly designed auction, for example, can result in the seller getting a higher price than if he had sold at a fixed price. In general, buyers and sellers will respond to the rules, and in most cases these responses can be predicted. For example, bidders in an English auction are likely to go on bidding until they reach the highest price they are willing to pay. As a consequence, the effects of the choice of rules on outcomes can also be predicted.

This relationship between the design of trading mechanisms and their outcomes is the subject of chapters 6 (focusing on direct negotiations), 7 (focusing on auctions) and 8 (focusing on exchanges). But this chapter takes the mechanisms *as given* and asks: given the variety of trading mechanisms in business-to-business e-commerce, what factors will determine the choice of firms of what mechanisms to use?

The answer to this question begins to emerge by assuming the simplest setting, where there is only one way to trade. What, *within a given single mechanism,* determines the profits of the participating firm? As before, from the viewpoint of a single firm participating in the trade mechanism, what matters is:

- the likelihood of finding someone with whom mutually beneficial trade is possible;
- the gains to the company from the trade. Specifically, these will depend on the actual transaction details—for instance the agreed price—and the costs of trade. Costs such as commission charged by market makers and possibly the cost of negotiations in terms of time and manpower can often be very large.

But, although firms care only about their own profits, these will depend on the *overall efficiency* of the trading mechanism. The overall efficiency is the sum of gains to all participants from trading. Suppose that there are two buyers, one with willingness to pay $5 and the other $10. There are two sellers, one who is willing to accept any price above $2 and the other any price above $7. If the mechanism brings together the buyer who is willing to pay $5 with the seller that wants at least $7, then they will not trade—whatever the rules of the trading mechanism are. The best that can be achieved is to bring together the $5 buyer with the $2 seller and the $10 buyer with the $7 seller. Suppose that the first pair traded at a price of $3 and the second pair traded at a price of $8; then the overall efficiency is $6 (sum of surpluses), minus any trading costs, e.g. commission or opportunity costs in terms of time spent negotiating.

This example can be used to explain the relationship between individual gains and overall efficiency. Suppose, for example, that a different trading mechanism still brings the same two pairs of buyers and traders together, but the final prices are different, say $4 and $9. The overall efficiency is the same (assuming all costs are also kept the same), but the individual gains all change. The prices are higher and so sellers are better off in the second mechanism and buyers are worse off. Another trading mechanism which matches buyers and sellers differently will result in only one pair (the $10 buyer and $2 seller) trading. Such a mechanism will be less efficient. It will also affect individual gains—the buyer and seller who do trade have a higher surplus to split. If they agree a price of $6, then they are both better off than in any of the previous two mechanisms, but clearly the other two (who now do not trade at all) are worse off.

This simple example illustrates not only how to compute total gains from trade but also why total gains have in general only an indirect effect on traders. They will naturally be more concerned with their own share of the surplus.

The efficiency of a trading mechanism depends in general on two factors:

1. the matching technology, that is, the costs, or inefficiencies, associated with the process of bringing together buyers and sellers; and
2. the actual amount of trade compared with the potential amount of trade.

The first point is relatively straightforward. Consider, for example, a trading mechanism that matches pairs of buyers and sellers, and lets them negotiate directly with each other. After some time, all buyers and sellers who could not agree a deal are again matched in pairs (not with the same person they were matched with before) and allowed to negotiate. Again, after some time the remaining buyers and sellers are matched in pairs, and the process is repeated many times, perhaps until everyone trades. Compared with centralized markets where all trade takes place simultaneously, the matching technology of such a trading mechanism is clearly inefficient because of the length of time many buyers and sellers will have to spend before trading, and the high negotiation costs they will incur.

The second point requires more explanation. Efficiency is also determined by the amount of trade that actually takes place between buyers and sellers for whom trade is possible. In most trade situations, each party knows only the worth of the deal to itself, not to the others. For example, the buyer will normally not know what the seller is willing to pay. Moreover, the seller is unlikely to reveal this value to the buyer. But the fact that traders have this "private information" may then result in the trading process being inefficient. For example, a buyer may reject a price that is essentially acceptable to her (that is, it is higher than the worth of the deal) because she thinks she can get a better price. But this may lead to negotiations breaking down and the object not being exchanged, despite the fact that—in theory—the traders could have agreed a price that is acceptable to both. The following section elaborates more on this point and explains one of economic theory's most important results on the efficiency of bilateral negotiations.

The inefficiency of bilateral negotiations

In a seminal paper, Roger Myerson and Mark Satterthwaite (1983) show that this uncertainty is closely connected with the inefficiency of bilateral trade. In their analysis, there are two individuals: a seller who owns a product and a buyer who wishes to buy it. The seller knows the valuation of the product—the lowest price for which he will agree to sell it, X—and the buyer knows hers—the highest price he is willing to pay, Y—but neither knows the other's valuation. Efficiency requires that, if Y is greater than X, then trade should occur because there is scope for mutually beneficial trade: the buyer's valuation of the product is higher than the seller's. Any price between X and Y is good for both of them. In the example above, X equals $4 and Y equals $10 so any price between $4 and $10 is beneficial and should in theory be acceptable to both.

But it may happen that, even when Y is greater than X, privately informed traders will fail to reach an agreement. To illustrate this problem, consider the following bilateral trading mechanism. The buyer announces the highest price she is willing to pay for the product, and the seller simultaneously announces the lowest price he is willing to accept. The mechanism (the "rules") then works as follows: if the price announced by the buyer (Y') is greater than or equal to the price announced by the seller (X'), trade will take place, and the price is set to the average between the two announcements. But if the buyer is offering less than the seller is demanding, no trade will take place.

This simple mechanism would be efficient if both the buyer and the seller truthfully reported their valuations, that is, if the buyer reports Y', which is the same as Y, and if $X'=X$. But this is clearly not in their best interest. For example, the buyer, knowing the rules, would always report Y' that is smaller than Y because this would lead to a better price for her. Similarly, the seller would report X' that is greater than X.

Returning to the example above, the seller will report not his true valuation, $4, but a higher value. Similarly, the buyer will announce a price less than $10. Both buyer and seller will be fully justified in doing so—they are acting rationally. But this rational behavior can lead to an inefficient outcome. For example, if the seller reports $7 while the buyer reports $6, then no trade is possible—despite the fact there the "real" X is greater than the "real" Y. More generally, when Y is greater than X but not by a huge amount, then it becomes likely that Y' will be smaller than X', and no trade will take place. Hence, even though the buyer values the object more than the seller does— Y is greater than X—no trade will occur.

Is the inefficiency a byproduct of the specific mechanism described above, or is it a necessary feature of bilateral negotiations between privately informed traders? Perhaps if the rules are changed so that the traders can make offers and counter-offers, the outcome will become more efficient? This is the question that Myerson and Satterthwaite set out to answer. Is there a trading mechanism, a set of rules, that can *ensure* trade every time Y is greater than X, assuming only that both the buyer and the seller will act rationally?

But Myerson and Satterthwaite find that this inefficiency is in fact very general. It is not possible to design a bilateral trading mechanism that ensures that trade occurs every time Y is greater than X (in economic terms, a mechanism that is *ex ante* efficient), and where both the buyer and the seller are guaranteed not to make a loss. The second part of the statement may seem strange at first. The idea is simple, though. It *is* possible to give both traders the right incentives to reveal their true valuations. But this may involve some penalties in some cases, and it is possible that one or both traders will end up losing money. These types of mechanism are of no use, since no one will choose to participate in such a mechanism.

Another way to interpret this result is to say that efficient mechanisms simply do not exist. This is a very strong result, since obviously no one can imagine all possible bilateral trade mechanisms. Still, it is clear that there is a limit to the efficiency of what can be achieved using any such mechanism.

As an illustration of the size of this inefficiency, consider the following example. Suppose that both the seller's and the buyer's valuations are between 0 and 1. The buyer knows her own valuation but knows nothing about the seller's valuation except that it is between 0 and 1. The buyer believes that it can take any of the values in this interval with equal probabilities, and the seller has the same beliefs about the buyer's valuation, X. So any point in the rectangle in Figure 4.3 corresponds to a pair of valuations, X and Y. Efficiency requires that every time $Y>X$, that is at any point above the diagonal line $Y=X$, trade will occur.

But for exactly the same example, Myerson and Satterthwaite show that the best that *any* mechanism can do is to ensure trade if Y is greater from X by at least $\frac{1}{4}$, that is, only at points lying above the broken diagonal line. It is not possible to design a mechanism so that trade occurs if $Y>X$ but $Y<X+\frac{1}{4}$, that is, in the entire area that lies above the line $Y=X$ and below the broken line. It is easy to see from Figure 4.3 that this is a considerable part of the area for which $Y>X$. In fact, it represents nearly half of the cases for which trade is possible. More formally, if X and Y are independently uniformly distributed over the interval 0 to 1, then the conditional probability that $Y<X+\frac{1}{4}$, given that $Y>X$, is 0.4375 (nearly 44 percent).

Figure 4.3 illustrates the degree of efficiency that can be achieved by any bilateral trading mechanism as proved by Myerson and Satterthwaite.

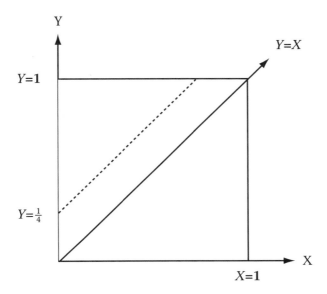

Figure 4.3: An illustration of the inefficiency of bilateral negotiations

Does this mean that all markets are inefficient?

So bilateral negotiations between privately informed traders are always inefficient. But does this negative result extend to the interactions of more than one seller and buyer? In markets with many buyers and sellers, such as the call auction markets used in financial markets like the New York Stock Exchange, traders submit bids to the market maker—or possibly to a computerized system. The market maker, whether human or electronic, then determines a market clearing price based on these bids. All buyers who bid above the clearing price trade with all sellers bidding below the clearing price. For example, assume that there are five buyers and five sellers. The sellers submit the following bids: 10, 8, 8, 6 and 1; and the buyers submit the bids 2, 3, 5, 7 and 9. Then the market clearing price will be set somewhere in the interval 6 and 7, because this is where the demand and supply curves cross. This implies that the sellers who bid 6 and 1 will trade with the buyers who bid 7 and 9.

Do traders in such markets have incentives to manipulate the outcome by not reporting their true valuations? The answer is that they do, but that these incentives are very small, and for all practical purposes traders in markets of many buyers and sellers are "truth telling". The intuition for this result is as follows. A trader, say a buyer, submits a bid. This bid will determine whether she will trade. (She will trade only if her bid is higher than the clearing price.) It may also affect the clearing price. Her bid will affect the clearing price if she happens to be the "marginal" buyer, that is the buyer located on the bit of the demand curve that crosses the supply curve. (In the example above, the buyer who bid 7 is the marginal buyer.) The probability of being the marginal buyer is therefore proportional to the total number of buyers in the market. And if there are many buyers, this probability is very small.

So what bid should a rational buyer submit? With a large probability, the buyer will *not* be the marginal buyer and therefore will not affect the clearing price. So she can take the price as given (although of course she does not know this in advance). In this case, it is easy to see that the buyer's optimal strategy is to tell the truth. If she bids too little then she may lose out on profitable trade. (For example, if her real valuation is $7 but she bids $5, then she will not trade if the clearing price turns out to be $6.) If she bids too much, then she may end up trading at a loss. (If she bids $9 and the clearing price is $8, then she will have to trade and make a loss of $1.)

With a small probability, the buyer will be the marginal buyer, and her bid will affect the clearing price. In this case, the buyer may benefit from shading her bid upwards. But as the number of traders increases, her incentive to do so is outweighed by her incentive to tell the truth in case she is not the marginal buyer. And so the inefficiency associated with private information becomes smaller.

It is clear that Myerson and Satterthwaite's result is specific to bilateral negotiations and does not extend to markets with many buyers and sellers. In fact, such markets—or exchanges—can be efficient both in terms of the matching technology, and in terms of overcoming the problems associated with private information. Exchanges bring together many potential buyers and sellers in a central place—whether physical or online—where all trade can take place quickly. In economic terms, bringing together many buyers and sellers is known as providing *liquidity*.

Bearing in mind these results about the efficiency of different mechanisms, we now turn back to our original question. What determines the decisions of buyers and sellers as to what mechanism to use?

Choosing between auctions and negotiations

Standard English auctions, where the price rises continuously until there is only one bidder left willing to pay, are generally considered a good way to maximize revenues for sellers. Similarly, reverse, or procurement, auctions are considered a useful way to minimize costs for buyers. A properly designed auction can select the buyer with the greatest willingness to pay (or, in a reverse auction, the seller who is willing to sell at the lowest price). Instead of guessing how much buyers are willing to pay, as sellers are forced to do when they use a fixed price scheme, by using an auction, the seller is forcing buyers to name their own prices, hence revealing how much they think the item is worth. This is why, for example, U.S. takeover laws favor auctions: the board of a company that is being sold is legally bound either to use an auction or to provide a good enough reason to its shareholders why it chose not to use one.

In an English auction, there is a simple optimal strategy for bidders: continue to bid either until you win or until the price exceeds your maximum willingness to pay. The result is that the bidder with the highest valuation wins the auction. English auctions are particularly popular online: the vast majority of web auctions are either English auctions or auctions based on the English auction rules. This may be because, by using a standard, well-known auction format, the seller (or buyer) is able to attract a large number of potential buyers (or sellers). By operating around the clock, Web-based auctions allow bidders from different time zones, who may be physically very far apart, to bid. So, by conducting an English auction on the web, the seller (or, in a procurement auction, the buyer) can reasonably expect to increase the size of demand and sell to the buyer with the highest willingness to pay. These are very good reasons to choose an auction.

But just how do auctions compare with other methods of selling and procuring? Once the seller commits himself to an auction, he has no control over the price. He will have to accept the highest bid (unless it is lower than any reserve price he has set, i.e. the minimum price he is willing to accept). Perhaps the seller would be better off negotiating with a small number of potential buyers where he has full control over the negotiating process, including the final price? This seems reasonable. But a more careful analysis leads to a different conclusion: the seller is better off in an auction as long as he is able to attract at least one extra bidder.

The comparison between auctions and negotiations was first carried out by Jeremy Bulow and Paul Klemperer (1996). Their paper compares the expected revenue for a seller using an English auction with $n+1$ potential buyers with the highest attainable revenue for the same seller negotiating with n buyers. They find that the seller is better off in the first case. Similarly, a buyer is better off conducting a reverse English auction with $n+1$ potential sellers than by directly negotiating with n potential sellers.

Another way of understanding this result is to think of a seller conducting an English auction with n potential buyers. The seller can now choose between having an extra bidder or sticking with the bidders he already has but changing the rules in whatever way he likes. For example, he may carry out an English auction with these n buyers, and then, instead of simply accepting the highest bid, start negotiating with the bidder that made this bid. This is of course a very unrealistic scenario, since it is unlikely that any bidders will agree to participate in this kind of negotiation.

What makes Bulow and Klemperer's result so powerful is the fact that, even if such strange methods of negotiations are allowed, the seller is still better off opting for the English auction with the extra bidder. In their own words,

> remember that our analysis assumed that a seller could negotiate optimally, making credible commitments of the sort that might not be possible in real life, and we also assumed that bidders had no bargaining power in a negotiation. We therefore believe that our basic result does not overstate the efficiency of auctions relative to negotiations.

Moreover, this result implies that the seller is better off using an English auction as long as the number of bidders in the auction is larger than the number of potential buyers he can directly negotiate with. This is true because, if the seller is better off in an auction with $n+1$ bidders, then he is clearly even better off in an auction with $n+2$, $n+3$, etc. sellers. This makes the result particularly relevant for web-based auctions where, by choosing to use an auction, the seller is already likely to attract more bidders.

A closer look at what is being compared is useful. Suppose that the seller is carrying out an English auction with n potential buyers. What are the gains from one extra bidder? This extra bidder will make a difference only in two cases.

- First, if she has a higher valuation than any of the existing *n* bidders, she will win the auction and the revenue for the seller will increase.
- Second, if her valuation is in between the current highest and second highest valuations, then, although she will not win the auction, she will still have a positive impact on the outcome.

Suppose that the current highest valuation is $100, and the current second highest is $80. Then the person who places a value of $100 on the item will win it, and she will pay slightly over $80 for it, say $81. (The exact figure will depend on the increments used by the auctioneer.) Now suppose that the extra bidder values the product at $90. The person who values it by $100 will still win the auction but will now have to pay over $90 for it. So the revenues for the seller increase.

In all other cases—that is, when the new bidder's valuation is lower than the current second highest valuation—the extra bidder will have no effect on the outcome. Still, considering all cases, the value of an extra bidder is higher than the extra revenue that the seller can extract through negotiations. In other words, the value of negotiating skill is small relative to the value of additional competition.

Bulow and Klemperer's result provides the first insight into the choice of trading mechanisms in business-to-business e-commerce. Auctions dominate negotiations; competition is more important than investing in better negotiating skills. As long as the seller can carry out an auction, he should do so. Similarly, buyers have strong incentives to carry out a reverse auction.

But auctions are not always possible, especially for goods and services for which there are, at any given stage, many buyers and sellers. In these circumstances it is not always possible for an individual buyer to determine her trading mechanism, because she must take into account what the other buyers are doing. The scope of the analysis therefore needs to be expanded to deal with the interactions of many buyers with many sellers.

Choosing between exchanges and negotiations

A substantial proportion of business e-commerce is expected to take place through electronic exchanges. This seems reasonable since, compared with existing business media, such as using the telephone to negotiate with a small number of approved suppliers, electronic exchanges provide more liquidity and flexibility. They also reduce the transaction costs of trading and offer greater efficiency overall. This is particularly true when the good or service is homogeneous. For example, Forrester Research found that the percentage of trade through electronic exchanges was substantially higher for utilities (91 percent) and electronics (74 percent) than for heavy industries (6 percent), where the details of each trade tend to differ.

Despite these obvious advantages from trading via electronic exchanges, it is not clear whether each single buyer and seller can expect to gain from participating in these new markets. Moreover, the decision to continue to trade in the "old way" or switch to trading via exchanges will depend on the choices made by the other buyers and sellers. This problem is addressed by Zvika Neeman and Nir Vulkan (2000) in a paper on the incentives of buyers and sellers to trade with their suppliers and clients via electronic exchanges. The main result of their analysis indicates that, although not all traders will benefit at first from trading in these new exchanges, eventually all trade will be conducted through exchanges.

The set-up that Neeman and Vulkan use is as follows. There are many privately informed traders who have access to two forms of trade:

1. direct negotiations with a small number of buyers and sellers;
2. a competitive market with a relatively large number of buyers and sellers.

If they choose negotiations, they have full control over the outcomes. In other words, they are free not to commit as long as they are not happy with the terms offered to them. If they trade via the electronic exchange, however, they will interact with a larger number of potential trade partners, but the scope for exercising control over final agreements will be significantly smaller. In fact, for the most part, all that businesses can do in such markets is to place an offer or a bid.

Recall from the discussion of the efficiency of markets above that, when trading on an exchange, each trader takes the price, for all practical purposes, as given. This is either because their own bid is unlikely to affect the price or because the bid has only a very small effect on the price. Suppose that traders expect the market price to be equal to p. The first observation is that no trade at an expected price that is different from p can occur through any form of direct negotiations because either the buyer or the seller would be better off transacting via the exchange. Based on this, Neeman and Vulkan prove the following results.

- First, buyers with a high willingness to pay and sellers with a low cost will prefer the greater liquidity afforded by exchanges, *even if they are optimistic* about what they can achieve through direct negotiations.
- Second, this leads to a complete unraveling of direct negotiations, so that ultimately, all "serious" buyers and sellers opt for participation in exchanges. The intuition for the result is that, since a single trader's willingness to pay hardly affects the price in a large exchange, exchanges protect "weak trader" types against paying high prices if they happen to be buyers and accepting low prices if they happen to be sellers. In contrast, under direct negotiations, because of their weakness, weak buyer types are likely to pay relatively high prices and weak seller types are likely to be forced to accept low prices. As weak types of buyers and sellers opt for trading via the exchange, the price remains relatively unaffected. In contrast, as weak types of buyers and sellers opt out of direct negotiations, the distribution of the remaining buyer and seller types puts relatively more weight on relatively stronger types, which again forces those buyers and sellers with relatively weak types to pay higher prices and accept low prices, respectively.
- Finally, this unraveling of direct negotiations eventually pushes all "serious" traders—buyers with willingness to pay above the market price and sellers with costs below the market price—toward trading on the exchange. Once all serious traders decline to engage in direct negotiations, no other trader can profitably trade that way.

The following example illustrates the argument. Consider an environment with four traders, two buyers and two sellers. Each buyer wants to buy, and each seller wants to sell, one unit of some homogeneous product. One buyer's willingness to pay for the product is 10, whereas the other buyer's willingness to pay is 2; and one seller's cost of producing the product is 8, whereas the other seller's cost is 0.

If all the traders trade in a market where they behave as price-takers, then any price p between 2 and 8 can serve as a market clearing price (because this is where the "demand" and "supply" curves will cross[1]). Suppose, for simplicity, that the price that prevails in the market is $p=5$. The buyer with the willingness to pay 10 trades with the seller whose cost is 0, and both obtain a payoff of 5 (10–5 for the buyer and 5–0 for the seller). The other buyer and seller do not trade in the market and each obtain a payoff of 0.

Suppose on the other hand that the traders engage in direct negotiations with each other. Suppose further that this negotiation assumes the following form: a first stage of random matching between the buyers and sellers, and a second stage of "split-the-surplus" bargaining. (Notice that this is already a very optimistic description of direct negotiations: first, the Myerson–Satterthwaite result indicates that the traders may not agree at all, depending on their beliefs about each other's willingness to pay; and second, this is a very inefficient matching technology—in reality, negotiations will be time-consuming and costly. In economic terms, some of the surplus will be lost because of these inefficiencies.) But even under these "rosy" assumptions about the outcomes of bargaining, traders will still prefer to switch to markets. If bargaining inefficiencies are taken into account, the results therefore become even stronger.

Returning to the example, the expected payoff to the buyer whose willingness to pay 10 from direct negotiations is $\frac{1}{2}[10-(10+8)/2]+\frac{1}{2}[10-(10+0)/2]=3$. This is because, with probability $\frac{1}{2}$, the buyer is matched with the seller whose cost is 8, trades at the price 9 (by splitting the difference between 10 and 8), and obtains a payoff of 1. With probability $\frac{1}{2}$, the buyer is matched with the seller whose cost is 0, trades at the price 5 (by splitting the difference between 10 and 0), and obtains a payoff of 5. So on average, the payoff from direct negotiations is 3.

The expected payoff to the buyer whose willingness to pay 2 is $\frac{1}{2}[2-(2+0)/2]=\frac{1}{2}$ by similar computations. (There is only

---

1   The demand curve is as follows. For any price less than 2 the demand is 2. For any price between 2 and 10 the demand is 1. (There is only one buyer who will willing to pay any price in this interval.) For all prices greater than or equal to 10 the demand is zero. Similarly, the supply function is 1 for prices up to 8 and 2 for all prices above 8. So for any price below 2 demand exceeds supply, and for any price above 8 supply exceeds demand. Supply equals demand (both equal to 1) for any price between 2 and 8.

one case to be considered here, since when this buyer is matched with the seller whose cost is 8, no trade takes place.) Similarly, the expected payoff to the seller whose cost is 8 is $\frac{1}{2}$ and the expected payoff to the seller whose cost is 0 is 3.

Obviously, the buyer with a high willingness to pay and the seller with the low cost (the "weak" types) are better off in the exchange compared with direct negotiations. Even if they alone switch to trading through the exchange, they are still better off as they can trade at the competitive equilibrium price $p=5$. But once they switch, the remaining buyer and seller become worse off since they lose their ability to trade.

Neeman and Vulkan show that, if there are many buyers and sellers, this argument can be *repeated*. That is, at each stage more buyers and more sellers will switch to the market, because their expected payoff, *conditional on the fact that all "weak" traders have switched to trading via markets,* is higher in the market. This can be repeated until there are no longer any opportunities for trading outside the marketplace.

Hence, not only do markets dominate negotiations in terms of efficiency, they are also the only reasonable long-term outcome when traders can choose their medium of trading. Since this is exactly the case in business-to-business e-commerce, this result has important implications for the future of electronic markets. This theoretical finding seems already to be supported by data: a recent study by Fiona Morton, Florian Zettelmeyer and Jorge Silva-Risso (2001) looks at a large dataset of transaction prices for new cars purchased online and offline. The authors conclude that "the Internet is disproportionaletly beneficial to those who have personal characteristics that put them at a disadvantage in negotiations", which correspond to what Neeman and Vulkan call the "weak" traders type.

The speed with which exchange sites for bonds (such as Cantor Fitzgerald's eSpeed and TradeWeb, owned by Lehman Brothers, Merrill Lynch) and energy (like the Intercontinental Exchange—ICE) became major players in their respective markets is also consistent with the predictions of the model: in both markets, direct negotiations were the dominant mode of trade before the exchanges began trading.

Choosing between exchanges and auctions

The above discussion of trading mechanisms surveys the choices between negotiations and auctions and between negotiations and exchanges. It is also worth thinking about the choice between auctions and exchanges. Sellers can expect to get higher prices in an auction because, in effect, they can act as monopolists. But this is true only if there is sufficient competition. More specifically, if no bidders participate in the auction, or if only one does, then the seller could very well have been better off selling through an exchange.

On the other hand, buyers are unlikely to buy through an auction if they expect to pay more than in the exchange. The final outcome remains an open question, but it seems reasonable to assume that the only stable outcome (that is, the only equilibrium in the game where buyers and sellers first choose which mechanism to trade through and then trade) is where all trade occurs via exchanges. The Neeman–Vulkan result is therefore likely to extend to this case too.

Once more, this illustrates the competitive pressure toward trading though exchanges (or many-to-many markets). If a growing proportion of trade between companies takes place through e-commerce, then it is likely that exchanges will become, in the long run, the dominant trading mechanism.

B2B E-COMMERCE IN PRACTICE: EXOSTAR

Up until this point, the discussion assumes that all traders are "equal", i.e. that there are no obvious major players. But important issues arise when the major players in an industry are themselves setting up electronic exchanges. On the one hand, suppliers may be reluctant to participate in such marketplaces since they are likely to favor the major players, who are also the market makers. On the other hand, the finding that efficiency requires trade to take place through exchanges indicates that at least some firms will benefit from switching, and once they do the incentives to switch to the exchange increase further for many of the remaining players. The following example of B2B e-commerce in practice illustrates this dilemma for suppliers and corporate buyers in the aerospace and defense industries.

In March 2000, the creation of an Internet trading exchange for the global aerospace and defense industries was announced. The founding partners were Boeing, Lockheed Martin, BAE and Raytheon, all leading aerospace manufacturers. These firms were to create and spin off the exchange as an independent company. It was named Exostar, and was based on Microsoft and Commerce One's MarketSite Portal solution.

Background on the industry

The global aerospace and defense industry has annual sales of more than $400 billion. Exostar's founding participants make purchases amounting to over $70 billion per year, involving more than 37,000 suppliers, hundreds of airlines and several national governments.

Yet, despite the large sales revenues generated by the industry, it suffers from very flat earnings growth. This has occurred since the defense cut-backs of the 1990s, which forced companies to curtail expansion and resulted in a great deal of consolidation within the industry. The only solution remaining for defense and aerospace contractors was to cut costs in order to increase their margins and raise earnings growth. This is not an easy way to increase earnings.

Aim of Exostar

The aim of Exostar is to bring together the vast array of players in the aerospace and defense industry in one virtual marketplace. By linking the buying and selling of parts and supplies online, benefits are expected to come from reduced transaction costs, aggregated buying power and lowered prices via auctions and increased competition.

The industry now

The global aerospace and defense industry is currently complex and fragmented. Certain suppliers operate online while others do not. Each supplier has its own catalog and ordering systems, which makes product search, price comparison and ordering a costly and labor-intensive process.

Several Internet start-ups are currently attempting to establish a foothold in the rapidly growing online aerospace market before the established bricks-and-mortar companies get their Internet exchanges running. Companies such as Boeing, Honeywell and Raytheon will seek to use their established names and supply chain relationships to ensure that their emerging Internet exchanges become successful. Examples of such e-marketplaces are EverythingAircraft.com, a wholly owned subsidiary of Raytheon Company, and MyAircraft.com, led by Honeywell. EverythingAircraft.com claims to be the aviation industry's portal for the buyers and suppliers of aircraft parts. It offers access to electronic catalogs of manufacturers and is aiming to be a one-stop shop for the purchasing of aircraft parts. MyAircraft also offers access to online catalogs and aims to help supply chain partners to integrate their planning and operations in order to improve the transaction process.

As many as a dozen e-commerce B2B web portals have emerged over the last few years. But as the aerospace and defense dot.com landscape is quickly filling with potential competitors, not all are expected to survive. An illustration is AviationX, one of the initial independent B2B Internet parts exchanges in the industry, which was forced to suspend efforts to build an online parts warehouse after it failed to attract customers.

Services provided by Exostar

Exostar offers several tools to aid transactions and offer support to the aerospace and defense industry:

- transaction tools;
- collaborative tools;
- supply chain management tools;
- community services.

Transaction tools

Electronic catalogs allow buyers to search for products and suppliers online. General product information, services and specifications as well as customer codes and lists are all accessible via Exostar. Orders and issue releases can be dealt with through the exchange. In addition, there are facilities to track the status of any particular order, send advanced shipping notices and manage any amendments. Finally, the invoicing and payment of orders can be conducted via the exchange.

Both forward and reverse auctions are available through the exchange. Forward auctions enable sellers to move surplus stocks by advertising online. Reverse auctions allow buyers to quote the price they are willing to pay for a product and then manage bids from multiple suppliers.

Collaborative tools

The collaborative tools available include program management, trading partner management and in-service support. Together these can result in improvements in the design of new parts, the reduction of waste in the supply chain and the shortening of cycle times. Innovations could thus be developed over a shorter time and at a lower cost than would otherwise be possible.

Supply chain management tools
By operating over the Internet, Exostar can offer services that enable coordination across the entire supply chain and at a low cost. These services include the planning of demand, supply and logistics, as well as supply network modeling. Thus, the various parties in the supply chain can share demand forecasts, inventory data and production plans. Since demand needs can then be forecast, suppliers can ensure that the right part is available at the right time to meet demand without the need to carry excess inventory.

Community services
The community services include the provision of industry news, electronic conferencing, product and service training, technical publications and access to an aerospace and defense library. Thus any industry participant can access up-to-date industry news and technical information.

Exostar aims to use these tools to address three main areas within the aerospace and defense industry:

1. non-production procurement;
2. the designing and building of aerospace and defense products;
3. the provision of spares and maintenance for airlines, aviation operators and defense businesses.

Non-production procurement Non-production procurement involves the purchasing of products and services, ranging from office supplies to plant maintenance. Procurement in this area is typically very labor intensive and involves a lot of paperwork. As a result, the time and cost involved with transactions are high. Any means of simplifying the process would thus benefit the company by reducing the time and transaction costs involved.

Exostar offers an online procurement alternative that automates such purchasing processes, thus resulting in potentially significant cost savings. The simplification of the procurement process occurs through several of Exostar's transactional capabilities, which enable the searching for and ordering of products to be done entirely through the exchange.

Designing and building aerospace and defense products Designing and building aerospace and defense products requires a great deal of program coordination between developers, manufacturers and suppliers. Program management in the aerospace and defense industry is an extremely complicated process that can span several years and involve anything up to several hundred companies.

Exostar facilitates interaction between these companies by providing a global marketplace through which new suppliers can be found and coordination between developer, manufacturer and supplier can be streamlined. In addition to its transactional tools, Exostar's collaborative tools enable the developers, manufacturers and suppliers on projects to be aligned in their program goals. The supply chain management tools further enable effective coordination across the entire supply chain.

Spares and maintenance Maintenance delays and errors are a constant concern within the aerospace and defense industry. Exostar provides online parts availability and pricing for approved suppliers. The location and ordering of vital parts can thus be carried out with minimal search time and fewer errors. Exostar's transaction and auction services facilitate this process.

Incentives for parties to join

Lowering costs is the main reason why companies would want to join Exostar. There are three main ways in which Exostar could benefit them. First, there is a huge potential to cut both the time it takes to conduct a transaction and the amount of paperwork involved. Second, the companies involved could aggregate purchasing requirements to obtain lower prices from suppliers. Thirdly, they could use online auctions, both normal and reverse, to encourage greater transparency and lower prices. These obviously offer different advantages to buyers and sellers.

Suppliers

Exostar brings together many of the elements necessary for suppliers to operate efficiently and at reduced cost. Companies, products and information are brought together on the virtual marketplace.

Such a global marketplace offers suppliers, and especially smaller suppliers, broader market reach and access to more potential customers. In addition, there is clearer visibility of customer demand, which enables suppliers to produce according to more accurate information than is usually available.

There is therefore the potential for revenue growth while at the same time reducing sales and marketing costs.

In such a marketplace the ordering process can be standardized and streamlined, thus reducing the costs and time involved in transactions. Automating the purchasing system can additionally help reduce delivery cycle times and inventories. Inventories can further be reduced through the online auctions available to move excess parts. Insiders suggest that the costs of processing purchase orders could fall by up to 90 percent while average order cycle times could be reduced by up to 50 percent. Therefore significant benefits are potentially available to suppliers by operating through Exostar.

However, most of the 37,000 industry suppliers have been cautious about joining Exostar, or for that matter any exchange. Some believe that an exchange, being led by the big companies, will not be able to remain neutral when it comes to setting ground rules. However supply companies, especially the smaller ones, may feel some pressure to join Exostar since their primary customers are the large aerospace companies such as Boeing and BAE.

Recently however, the competing trade exchange MyAircraft has been given a great boost. MyAircraft is owned by three of the world's largest aerospace suppliers: United Technologies, Honeywell International and BFGoodridge. It has recently been joined by nine of the world's biggest airlines, including American Airlines, British Airways and Air France. This is the first time that buyers and sellers in the industry have joined forces in a trade exchange. The site could ultimately handle a combined $75 billion procurement budget, as compared with Exostar's potential $71 billion. This could shift supplier incentives away from joining Exostar.

Buyers
Exostar offers many capabilities that facilitate the interaction of buyers and suppliers on a global scale. The virtual marketplace common to all parties provides the opportunity to interact and form relationships with all companies in the supply chain.

The marketplace provides easy access to price and product availability. Up-to-date inventory data from a range of suppliers enables companies to reduce the time required to search for necessary products and to compare prices. Access to pricing and product availability could, it has been said by insiders, reduce parts procurement by up to 10 percent.

The opportunity to standardize ordering processes can result in large savings of time and transaction costs, while reducing the possibility of error. The elimination of paper-based processes makes ordering less labor-intensive. Maintenance costs can also be cut through the ability to standardize and streamline ordering.

With aerospace's relatively static figures, many aircraft makers will find potential benefits in joining such an exchange in order to help reduce costs. Research has estimated that for every 1 percent saved in procurement costs, the aerospace industry could increase profits by 7 percent. That translates into big money for the major industry players like Boeing.

Despite this, several major companies were not part of Exostar at the outset. These included the U.S. firms Northrop Grumman and General Dynamics. It also excluded the European Aeronautical Defense & Space Co., which was formed by DaimlerChrysler's aerospace division, France's Aerospatiale Matra and the Spanish state firm Casa. The big aero-engine makers General Electric Co., Rolls-Royce and United Technologies unit Pratt & Whitney were similarly not included in Exostar.

One of the biggest uncertainties at the commencement of Exostar was Airbus, Boeing's rival in the commercial airline business. Airbus's European partners were merging to form the European Aeronautical Defense & Space Co. and would thus not be joining Exostar at the outset. But Airbus gave the exchange a boost when in June 2000 it agreed to join. The result is that Exostar now includes the world's five largest aerospace companies as well as the largest manufacturers of commercial airliners, Boeing and Airbus. The five principal partners make up more than 70 percent of the $400 billion annual aerospace-related purchases and produce virtually all of the world's commercial airliners. The incentives to buyers to join such an exchange are thus very significant.

B2B exchange in the car industry: Covisint

It is interesting to compare the experience of Exostar to another very similar exchange—Covisint. The B2B online exchange Covisint was created jointly in February 2000 by the big three automakers, DaimlerChrysler, Ford Motor and General Motors. Their intention was to build a venture to operate a central public e-marketplace for the industry.

Upon its establishment, annalists had different opinions about its effect on suppliers and in turn on the success of the exchange. Some said that setting a giant online exchange, although planned to save costs, would eventually cause a squeeze on suppliers' prices—because on the web switching costs will be zero. Others said it might save costs to suppliers as well, and if the exchange were neutral it would encourage suppliers to use its facilities, save the costs of integrating with different online systems, and enable suppliers to compare prices among themselves, thus maintaining a high level of prices.

The incentives for buyers and sellers to join Covisint are very similar to those concerning Exostar—on one hand, such a giant exchange almost guarantees the success of trade; but on the other hand, the rewards, or payoffs, from trade, especially for suppliers, are likely to be less favourable since the owners are themselves big players in the market.

Interestingly, other sellers were also reluctant to join. For example, the VM(BMW) group decided to create its own private exchange. VW Group Supply is a private exchange, whose members include the Audi, Seat and Skoda brands, manufacturing plants in Germany, Spain, the Czech Republic, Brazil and Mexico, and numerous other associated companies, such as VW Financial Services. BMW, Honda, Robert Bosch, Toyota, Volkswagen and other manufacturers also began constructing their own multimillion-dollar private exchanges. These players prefer to trade in a lower-liquidity environment than take the risk of being "swallowed" by a giant exchange owned mainly by other companies.

Lessons from Exostar

- The market for the aerospace and defense industry is complex and fragmented, and so the advantages from trading online are potentially huge.
- As in many other markets, the main obstacle to efficient online trade is the lack of standardization. (We come back to this issue in more detail in chapter 8.)
- However, further obstacles may arise from the fact that a small number of major players are running the market.
- Nevertheless, the competitive pressure to use online many-to-many markets can ensure that others too will eventually prefer to use marketplaces like Exostar.

KEY ISSUES FOR B2B E-COMMERCE

What business buyers and sellers need to know

- The success of any trading mechanism will depend on the incentives of buyers and sellers to participate in it.
- The impact of these incentives in *aggregate* is also a key issue in the success of a trading mechanism.
- Bilateral trade is inherently inefficient. This inefficiency is caused by the strong incentives of traders to not tell the truth about their real valuations. It cannot be remedied by changing the rules of the trading mechanism.
- Exchanges are efficient in that the incentives of traders to lie become very small as the number of participants increases.
- Auctions dominate negotiations—competition is more important than investing in negotiating skills.
- Exchanges dominate negotiations—once all "weak" trader-types switch to exchanges, the incentives of other trader types to switch will increase. In the long run, no trade will occur through negotiations.
- In the long run, exchanges are also likely to dominate auctions.

PART II

DESIGNING E-COMMERCE
APPLICATIONS

Chapter 5

E-commerce and the Principles of Economic Engineering

Part I of this book analyzed existing e-commerce applications. These applications were treated as *given*, with economic theory used to make various predictions, such as who will be the main beneficiaries from using these applications. Part II, in contrast, no longer takes applications as given; instead, it seeks to explain how economic theory can be used to *design* and implement efficient e-commerce applications, with lessons from companies and market makers who have successfully built effective online market mechanisms.

Economic design is a vast field, and to cover it all would be beyond the scope of this book. The next three chapters therefore focus on three scenarios that are of particular importance to designers of e-commerce applications, the most common classes of designs in e-commerce:

- "one-to-one"—direct negotiations;
- "one-to-many"—auctions;
- and "many-to-many"—exchanges.

This chapter introduces the more general principles behind economic engineering. The basic idea is that it is possible to design protocols in such a way as to elicit certain behaviors from participating self-interested economic actors. By providing them with incentives to behave in certain ways, it is possible to design protocols or "rules" that are economically efficient. It is essential to provide incentives that not only get users to do what they are supposed to do but also ensure their participation in the first place. This means that the "rules of the game" must make sense and must be relatively easy to understand. And they must of course be based on the assumption of rationality that behavior will be driven by self-interest.

THE MOTIVATION FOR ECONOMIC ENGINEERING

Economic engineering is essentially a set of tools and principles that can be used to design the rules that then govern the interactions of self-interested economic actors, such as buyers and sellers (or possibly software programs acting on their behalf). Economic engineering, the practice of eliciting certain behaviors—such as truth telling—through incentive design, is by no means a new invention, although the field has been revolutionized in the last three decades by the introduction of game theory. The story of the judgment of King Solomon from the Old Testament can be thought of as a very early example:

> Two women came before King Solomon, each claiming to be the mother of a newborn baby. Both had given birth the previous night to baby boys, but one of the babies had died. One woman claimed that the other stole her baby, while the other claimed she had not. King Solomon had to make a difficult choice. To everyone's astonishment, he proposed to cut the baby in two and give each of the women one half of the baby. On hearing this judgment, the real mother pleaded with the King not to cut the baby, saying she preferred him to be taken from her than be killed. The other woman accepted the King's ruling. King Solomon then ordered the baby to be given to the first woman, saying she must be the real mother.

Why is this an example of economic engineering? The two women knew the truth but King Solomon did not. King Solomon (whom the Bible tells us is a good man) wanted the real mother to have the baby, and so his task was to design a mechanism, a ruling, that would reveal to him who the real mother was. And so he proposed an outrageous action promoting an immediate response from the real mother. King Solomon's ruling, or mechanism, elicited truth telling and he was therefore able to identify the baby's real mother. [1]

---

[1] If, however, the woman who was not the real mother took advice from an economist, she too would have pleaded with the King not to cut the baby (i.e. she would have imitated the actions of the real mother). And then the King would not know

Over the last three decades, since the introduction of formal, game theoretical analysis, rapid progress has brought the subject to an engineering-like state, where a large number of well understood mechanisms can be prescribed for a given situation. Electronic markets—whether direct negotiations, auction or exchanges—are a particularly good place to apply this theory, because the interactions between participants are regulated by the communication protocol. Since there are already rules in place, it seems wise to ensure that they are the "right" rules— the ones that will lead to efficient outcomes. Whether a given protocol for self-interested economic actors will lead to efficient outcomes typically depends on the underlying strategic structure of their interactions. Economic analysis of this structure, which first studies the set of equilibria, is therefore of particular relevance to engineering such protocols.

Economic design in automated e-commerce

Economic design is especially relevant for the automated interactions that are becoming more and more widespread as e-commerce continues to mature. Even in consumer applications, such as eBay, simple "proxy bidders" are used to facilitate a more efficient bidding process. Users tell their proxy the maximum they are willing to pay and the proxy then bids the lowest amount necessary to beat the current best price, as long as it is below the user-specified limit.

In business applications, automation is used for certain well-defined, repeated activities, such as the purchase of small-scale indirect materials, or scheduling. Automation is also used in applications where it is either not possible or cost-inefficient to use people. Bandwidth trading agents are a good example: software programs representing buyers (for example Internet service providers) and sellers (for example telecommunication companies who own the fiber optics) negotiate prices.

It would be difficult to use people to do the same job—the automated negotiators need to process a large amount of information very quickly (for example estimating demand every couple of seconds based on data and current consumption) to determine their willingness to pay, or reservation price. Nor would it be cost effective to employ a person for the job—prices are agreed for a few seconds at a time, and the average size of

who the real mother was. So it seems that King Solomon's "economic design" was not without flaws. Still, thankfully, it worked.

the contract is very small (a few cents at a time). Software programs are perfect for this type of application. They are computationally strong, and they cost nothing to run.

Automation in e-commerce involves a software program that acts independently in accordance with its user's interests. Technically speaking, this is a pre-programmed algorithm acting on real-time data. As such, it corresponds exactly to the game-theoretical notion of what *a strategy* is. More precisely, a strategy in game theory is a mapping from all possible histories and information sets to actions. Once a player picks a strategy, he knows what to do in any given set of circumstances.

This suggests that game theory strategies might not describe very well how people behave in many cases. Casual observation makes it clear that people tend to make decisions as they go, or as events unfold. "We'll cross that bridge when we come to it." This may be sub-optimal in many cases, but nevertheless it is what people do. Designers of automated e-commerce, in contrast, instruct their programs *in advance* how to act, whatever happens. A software agent (or any real-time algorithm for that matter) *is* a "time-consistent" description of decision-making. Hence, game theory is probably more suitable for the study of automated interactions than it is for studying the interactions between humans. [2]

Rules of the game

The design of the communication protocol—the "rules of the game"—is central for e-commerce applications, whether they are used by people, software programs acting on their behalf, or a mixture of the two. These rules *are* the application. The list of e-commerce applications for which the economic design can be used to determine the communication protocol is enormous. Examples of such applications include:

- all types of Internet auction—consumer-to-consumer such as eBay, business-to-consumer such as uBid and Onsale, and business-to-business such as various commodity markets;

---

[2] This should not be seen as a criticism of game theory. Essentially, game theory is normative—it teaches how people should behave. But it also has a descriptive value. At least in some cases—especially if people care enough about the outcomes (for example if there are large sums of money involved) and if the rules are not too complicated—game theory predictions are consistent with observed behavior.

- markets for utilities, such as water and electricity;
- allocation of limited resources, such as bandwidth and data storage, within networks;
- scheduling among a number of self-interested groups, for example vehicle routing among independent dispatch centers, whether these belong to the same organization or not;
- markets for physical storage, for example the National Transportation Exchange (NTE) used for ground transportation, or similar such markets for trans-oceanic shipping storage;
- matching mechanisms for the labor market used by large organizations and manpower companies for recruitment and human resource management.

The design of the communication protocol is central to all these examples. A well designed protocol can make the difference between success and failure of the organization running this application.

One possibility is to use a centralized protocol, which dictates to each of the participants what to do. Using this approach, the performance of the application will then be guaranteed. But this comes at a huge price: users must agree to forsake their decision autonomy, and are not able to benefit from any information advantage that they may have. In most cases, they are very unlikely to do so.

For example, the private information of buyers and sellers (information that they have but their competitors or market counterparties do not) is a strategic asset, one that they are unlikely to give away for free. Moreover, since users can normally conduct their business by other means (for example by directly negotiating with clients), a centralized protocol is unlikely to appeal to users in the first place.

A decentralized protocol, where agents are free to make their own choices, is therefore the best way forward in most e-commerce applications. Although the protocol cannot dictate to users how to behave, it can provide them with the incentives to behave in certain ways. The chief goal of economic engineering is therefore *to elicit certain behavior from self-interested economic actors through the provision of appropriate incentives*. These incentives are provided through the rules of the game, that is, through the specification of the communication protocol.

ECONOMIC DESIGN IN PRACTICE

Economic institutions naturally evolve, but they are also sometimes designed. The theory described in this chapter has, in the last three decades, been put to practice in a variety of situations.

- At the national level, economic design is being used by governments to auction everything from railways to airwaves.
- At the level of the organization, the use of incentive schemes, such as share options and bonus payments, in employment contracts is now commonplace.
- At the individual level, many people participate in auctions and similar economic mechanisms. Since many of the goods traded on eBay are bought and sold by teenagers, [3] it is probably safe to say that the next generation will be even more familiar with auctions.

Auctions

Perhaps the best known examples of economic design are the telecoms auctions. Governments all over the world commissioned game theorists to design auctions to sell certain radio frequencies for the next generation of cellular telephones. The sums raised in these auctions were astronomical, and, at least in the United States and the United Kingdom, far beyond everyone's expectations.

In the U.K. auction, which was designed and tested by Paul Klemperer, Ken Binmore and a team from the Centre for Economic Learning and Social Evolution (ELSE) at University College London, and which raised £22.47 billion in the spring of 2000, the government sold five radiospectrum licenses. In the aftermath of the U.K. auction Binmore wrote the following, which is relevant to the ideas presented in this book:

> Although the revenue raised at the auction was enormous, the government's primary aim was actually to create a competitive and efficient industry. Competition was encouraged by restricting the four cellular telephone companies that currently operated in the United Kingdom to the four smaller licenses, reserving the largest and most valuable license for a new entrant. Efficiency then lay in assigning each license to the bidder who valued it most, because that

---

3   Toys are one of the most popular categories in eBay.

bidder would have the most effective business plan for the license.

But how does the government know who has the most valuable business plan? In the past, "beauty contests" were held. Government experts would consider the business plans submitted by the contending companies and hand out the licenses at a nominal price to the companies whose business plans seemed best. But such "beauty contests" have become discredited, not only because of suspicions of malpractice, but because it is only the contestants themselves who ... have the expertise necessary to distinguish good business plans from bad.

Economists have therefore long advocated the use of auctions instead. Auctions transfer the judgment on who should get a license to the real experts—the contestants themselves. There is no point, of course, in just asking the bidders who should get which license. Each bidder will simply say that their own business plan is best. Instead, the bidders must be given incentives that persuade them to reveal as much of the truth as is useful.

A carefully designed auction achieves this end by creating a competitive environment in which the bidders are forced to put their money where their mouth is. In the case of the U.K. telecoms auction, it turned out that 13 companies were willing to back up their ideas with very large sums of money indeed. Even the eight losers were willing to pay several billion pounds each.

What did the team of microeconomists do that Sotheby's could not do better? The U.S. government once hired Sotheby's to sell a number of satellite transponders. Sotheby's auctioned these off one by one as though they were old masters. In the event, the transponders, which were all pretty much the same, went for wildly different prices. It should be clear to anyone that such an outcome cannot possibly be efficient. The mistake made by both the U.S. government and Sotheby's was to imagine that an auction design that works well in one context will be sure to work well in another.

Using the mathematical techniques of game theory, it is possible to show that the rules of efficient auctions must be tailored closely to the economic environment. People are sometimes suspicious about the extent to which mathematical theorems are capable of predicting human behavior. In the case of auction theory, such fears turn out to be unfounded. When designs are tested in the laboratory, subjects, who are paid enough to capture their close attention, bid pretty much as the theory predicts after gaining a little experience.

Sotheby's mistake in selling the U.S. transponders sequentially is just one of the more obvious traps awaiting auctioneers who do not know auction theory. But it is instructive that the U.K. energy regulator OFGEM got itself into the same kind of trouble by forcing an inappropriate auction format on the sale of injection rights for North Sea gas into Transco's pipeline system.

Elsewhere, the same mistake was repeated in the telecoms industry when Swiss and Turkish governments auctioned radio spectrum licenses. The Turks had the bright idea of an additional twist that set the reserve price for the second of their two licenses equal to the price at which the first license was sold. As any game theorist would predict, one company then bid much more for the first license than it could possibly be worth if the company were to compete with a rival holding the second license. But the company had rightly figured that no rival would be willing to bid that high for the second license, which therefore remained unsold, leaving the company to operate a cosy little monopoly.

Economic design avoids such errors by using game theory to anticipate how the bidders' strategies will vary with the rules of the auction. It is then possible to predict the consequences of using each possible design. The auctioneer can then choose the design with an outcome that best matches the aims of the auction. (Binmore, 2000)

Economic design works for more situations than just auctions. And, although the telecoms auctions are excellent examples of economic design, they differ considerably from the design of most e-commerce protocols. While the principles are the same, a telecoms auction is a "one-off". Designers of these auctions had to work hard to get everything right because of the very large sums of money involved and the fact that, once the auction takes place, it is not possible to change the rules. In contrast, most e-commerce protocols are used repeatedly by agents while the typical size of the contract is small (for example a few cents per contract in the market for bandwidth, but the auction takes place every few seconds). A trial-and-error approach can, in most cases, be used to ensure that the design does elicit the required behavior from the participants.

Exchanges

A good example of economic design in "many-to-many" exchanges is the market for medical interns in the United States. Each year, a large number of students seek a place to do their medical internship. Students have their own preferences concerning hospitals. The more prestigious hospitals can expect to be in higher demand, as can hospitals in more desirable locations. It is common that students want to do their internship in their home town, where their family lives, or at least the same city as their partners. Of course, hospitals have preferences too: better students can reasonably expect to be in high demand; and hospitals may have different requirements from interns.

All of these considerations make the matching process between interns and hospitals very complex. Since the 1960s, game theoretical techniques have been used to design an algorithm (originally known as NIMP, the National Intern Matching Program) that matches the requirements of hospitals and students (see Roth, 1990). The algorithm needs to be efficient in that, once all matches take place, it should not be possible to make any change (for example by having some physicians swap their allocated places) without making someone worse off.

The incentives for interns to participate in the matching mechanism are also important. For example, the algorithm used in the 1960s and 1970s apparently did not deal well with the problem of couples: a large number of married couples found matches outside the NIMP, suggesting that the system was inefficient. Finally, the algorithm requires hospitals and interns to give their preferences. They should have the incentives to report their preferences truthfully. If, for example, students try to manipulate the system by entering the wrong information, then such strategic considerations can once more adversely affect the efficiency of the system. [4]

The market for medical interns is only one example of what economists call double-sided matching markets. Recruitment in general falls under this category. Since the Internet has become more widely available, the recruitment landscape has begun to change dramatically. Prior to the Internet, recruitment strategy was fairly basic, involving print, word of mouth, and perhaps some television and radio to bring in potential applicants and fill job vacancies. This was limiting in a many respects, since a recruiter had a fairly static talent pool to draw from.

The emergence of the Internet opened up a world of new possibilities to recruitment companies. The talent pool grew from regional to global. Recruitment firms could also expand their efforts to cover other industries, realizing that the relationships between them had become much more dynamic. Why recruit only nurses, when you could also recruit technicians and physical therapists at the same time?

Recruitment firms perform a matching mechanism: they match those looking for jobs with those offering jobs. The Internet has thus had a huge impact on the way the industry works, since the process can now operate much more efficiently. With larger pools of applicants and firms to draw from, recruiting agents can now match jobs and people more effectively. But the Internet not only benefits recruitment firms; it also empowers the job seeker. People now have more jobs to choose from through access to better information on vacancies. As a result, they can be more selective and raise their expectations of salary and benefits.

The Internet has also benefited companies looking for staff. When searching for good candidates, firms can now use their recruitment spending much more efficiently. Why spend $200 on a newspaper advertisements that reaches a small local audience, when that $200 could be spent reaching the entire

---

[4] The fact that players are not truthful does not necessarily mean that the outcome is not efficient. It is perfectly feasible that players manipulate their behavior strategically and the outcome is still efficient. For this to happen, however, all players must figure out how to behave, and in reality this can be quite complex. If only some of the players behave strategically, the situation can become very complex and it will be difficult to make any reasonable predictions about the outcome. If, on the other hand, players are provided with the necessary incentives to be truthful, then the equilibrium will be a realistic prediction of the outcome.

Internet? The cost-per-hire ratio over the Internet is anything up to 95 percent lower than equivalent recruitment through print advertising. Estimated hiring times have also been slashed, by up to two-thirds, through the automation of the hiring process. The consequence for companies is that they have a much wider reach in their recruitment now and so can afford to be far more discriminating in their hiring processes. To take full advantage of the possibilities of hiring over the Internet, 90 percent of large U.S. companies now recruit online.

DESIGNING INCENTIVES TO PARTICIPATE IN THE MARKET

In most e-commerce applications, participation is by choice. The designer of the protocol must therefore take account of the decisions of economic actors whether or not to participate.

Incentives to participate are especially important when potential participants are privately informed, for example when they alone know the quality of the goods they are selling, or their willingness to pay for an item. If the protocol is particularly attractive or unattractive to certain types of economic actor (for example those who sell high quality goods), then the problem of "adverse selection" might occur. Economic analysis suggests a number of measures that can be taken to combat this problem.

The problem of adverse selection

Adverse selection can occur when a protocol attracts certain types of participant more than other types. For example, suppose that an Internet auction house attracts a large proportion of dishonest sellers, perhaps because buyers pay in advance for the goods or because the auction house has no control or responsibility over the behavior of sellers. Buyers therefore face greater risk than from buying the same goods at a shop (where payment guarantees receiving the goods), or even than buying it in another auction house with a "no fraud" reputation. So they will purchase the product only if it is considerably cheaper than anywhere else. Anticipating this, honest sellers are therefore less likely to sell their goods via this auction house. The failure of the protocol designer to ensure honest behavior from her sellers could result in the commercial failure of her auction site.

Adverse selection occurs when there are information asymmetries, for example when the seller knows more about the quality of the goods or service that he is selling than his buyers.

The example most used by economists to explain the phenomenon is the market for second-hand cars or "lemons" (see Akerlof, 1970). But the same argument holds for any goods or service where the seller is better informed than the buyer. The information asymmetries in the case of second-hand cars are clear: the best way to determine the quality of a car is to drive it for a long period of time, and so the seller is likely to know the quality of the car and the buyer is not.

To illustrate the phenomenon, assume that there are only two kinds of cars: good cars and bad cars. Half of the cars on sale are bad, and the other half are good. Sellers value bad cars at $1,000 and good cars at $2,000 (that is, the seller of a good car will consider any price above $2,000, and the seller of a bad car will consider any price above $1,000). Buyers (for simplicity, they all have the same valuations) are willing to pay up to $1,100 for a bad car and $2,100 for a good car. If buyers could tell the quality of the car, then all cars would be sold: bad cars at prices between $1,000 and $1,100; and good cars at prices between $2,000 and $2,100.

But in the market for second-hand cars information is not symmetric. Buyers cannot differentiate between good and bad cars. So buyers are buying lotteries: with 50 percent probability they get a good car, and with 50 percent probability they get a bad car. A rational buyer will therefore never pay more than $1,600 for a car (1600 is the average of 1100 and 2100). But then sellers of good quality cars will prefer not to put their cars on sale because they value them at more than $2,000. After a while, buyers will figure out that only bad cars are being sold and will pay only up to $1,100. And so good cars will not be sold, despite the fact that there are buyers who are willing to pay more than the asking price for such cars.

Other examples of adverse selection can be found in insurance markets, where certain insurance policies may attract a non-proportional percentage of insurers with a higher than average chance of making a claim. For example, a medical insurance policy with special benefits for pregnant women is likely to be taken up by women planning to have babies in the next year or so. This increases the likelihood that the insurance company will have to pay up. Effectively, this will drive up the cost of the premium to a level that is likely to deter other women from taking up this insurance, resulting in a further increase in the premium. It can happen that the only premium possible (that is, in equilibrium) is even higher than the costs of paying directly for the medical treatment (because insurance companies need to make a profit, too). As a result, the policy as a whole will become not viable.

Adverse selection is particularly severe in e-commerce, because of the speed with which information spreads on the web. The "online storage" and "virtual desktop" market is a good example. In November 2001, Palm announced that it was closing its MyPalm.com service, which allowed Palm users to save files on a virtual drive. Companies such as Xdrive, iDrive, MediaDept and SwapDrive, which used to give 25–50MB of free storage space per user, have had to change their business models after being swamped with high storage users, storing huge video and music files. They now focus on business users only, and no longer provide free services.

It is therefore extremely important that the designer take appropriate measures to ensure that adverse selection does not occur in her application.

Solutions to the adverse selection problem

There are three general strategies that can be used to address the problem of adverse selection:

- group participation;
- signaling;
- screening.

Which of these is most appropriate will depend on the specific details of the application.

The first solution to adverse selection is to get groups rather than individuals to join the application. For example, if there is a joining fee, it can be reduced for groups over a certain size. Large groups are more balanced, since the distribution of those who are going to be heavy users is likely to be similar to that of the general population. (This is essentially the "law of large numbers": the statistical distribution of large samples resembles that of the whole population.) In fact, if it is possible to allow only group subscriptions, then the problem of adverse selection can be completely avoided. The online storage example above applies here. If Xdrive gives away free storage space, then it will be immediately swamped by teenagers swapping large video and music files. When they sign up a large consultancy firm, however, this is no longer the case. There will, of course, be heavy users in this firm, but the average user is far more likely to use the service to back up their files and presentations. By signing the whole firm, Xdrive is able to ensure a more normal pattern of use of its services.

The second solution to adverse selection is *signaling*. Returning to the second-hand cars example, if there were a credible way for sellers of high quality cars to signal this to potential buyers, then it would be in their best interests to do so (otherwise, no high quality cars would be sold in equilibrium).

Warranties offer just such a signaling device, because they tend to be more expensive for the seller of a bad quality car than for the seller of a high quality car. Cars with warranties are unlikely to be bad because the seller is liable for any repair work. By selling his car with a warranty, the seller therefore signals to the buyer that the car she is buying is of high quality. If, on the other hand, the car is sold "as is", the buyer concludes that it is of low quality, and therefore will want to pay less. By allowing participants to use credible signals, it becomes possible to overcome the problem of adverse selection. A signal is credible if it is more difficult (for example more expensive) for the "wrong" types to use it. Warranties are credible because they end up being more expensive for sellers of low quality goods.

The third solution to adverse selection is *screening*. Unlike signaling, which is an activity undertaken by the *informed* party, screening is a method that can be used by the *uninformed* party to try to overcome the problem of adverse selection. Since the protocol designer is normally the uninformed party (i.e. she does not know the true "types" of the user, whereas they do), this strategy is particularly suitable for e-commerce.

The basic idea is that the uninformed party offers a *menu* of contracts so that users sort themselves according to the contracts offered. A common example of screening is offering a number of pricing schemes. Telephone companies, for example, commonly use this strategy. If they offer the same price to everyone, they are likely to encounter adverse selection: a price set in accordance with average consumption will attract a non-proportional number of heavy users. So, rationally, the company needs to set the price higher than average usage would suggest. But this will drive low-frequency users out. In equilibrium, the inability of the firm to differentiate between consumers will result in a large segment of users being driven out of the market.

By offering a number of contracts, based on consumption,

the telephone company can avoid this problem. Customers, who know best how they are likely to use their phone, will select the package that suits them best. For example, low-frequency users will select low monthly charges with expensive per-call charges; heavy users will prefer to pay higher monthly charges but lower per-call charges. The firm now knows which is which, and is therefore able to set prices that maximize its profits, *given* the customer's type. This is clearly good for the company, but also good for consumers, since now everyone in the market is being served.

As with much economic design, the exact details matter. The various options must be set so that users will indeed pick the "right" contracts. For example, the price for low-frequency users should be set high enough to deter frequent users from choosing this option.

ENCOURAGING THE "RIGHT" BEHAVIOR

The design-related problems of participation are ones that occur *before* users begin to use an application. But sometimes information asymmetry can still cause significant problems *after* contracts are signed. This is true when the designer cannot observe or control the actions of the self-interested economic actors using their e-commerce applications. In many circumstances, the designer will not have access to the agents' private information, such as their willingness to pay or their real negotiating position.

The task of the designer is to provide participants with the right incentives to act according to their goals. For example, agents in a spot market for bandwidth can end up consuming too much bandwidth compared with what they really need, resulting in overall inefficiency. By charging prices based on aggregate demand, and not on available bandwidth (that is, prices go up with demand, regardless of whether the fiber optic cable can handle the current demand), the protocol can encourage less "greedy" behavior.

Similarly, in bargaining protocols, participants will try to pretend they are in a strong bargaining position, by suggesting, for example, that they have a very good outside offer or that their deadline to complete the bargain is distant. Again, this can result in overall inefficiency of the application, because of high negotiation overheads and unnecessary delays. Unless the protocol provides participants with adequate incentives to bargain truthfully, this problem is unlikely to disappear.

Optimal provision of incentives

Generally speaking, the designer can be viewed as seeking to provide incentives for participants to pick certain behaviors that are not initially in their self-interest, for example less "greedy" bandwidth consumption or truthful bargaining behavior. Although the general idea is simple enough, there are two problems that complicate the design task considerably.

- First, it may be difficult, and sometime impossible, for the protocol to monitor the behavior of the agents.
- Second, the outcome of the protocol may depend not only on the behavior of the agents: there may be additional factors affecting these outcomes, which are beyond the control of the agents. In the bandwidth consumption example, the suggested price mechanism is effective in deterring "over-consumption" behavior, but it also penalizes participants with real high demand.

The most common problem in designing protocols is *moral hazard*. This is best illustrated in the context of insurance markets, where the insurance contract can be viewed as a protocol. Most of the things against which people insure are at least partly under their own control. If a person is not insured, he is likely to take those precautions, and only those precautions, that save more than they cost (that is, the "right" precautions). Once an insurance policy is purchased, part of the cost of being careless and part of the benefit of taking precautions has been transferred to the insurance company; the cost to the insured is no longer the entire cost, so the result is no longer efficient. This externality is the basis for the problem of moral hazard; once someone is insured, someone else bears some of the cost of their actions.

Generally speaking, there are two lines of action against moral hazard:

- intense monitoring of the agents;
- provision of appropriate incentives.

Which of the two to use, and to what extent, will depend on the exact details of the underlying economic environment where the application is set. Intense monitoring may be the best option but it is rarely cost-effective. Returning to insurance markets, monitoring the actions of the insured is extremely costly. Intense monitoring is sometimes less costly in electronic markets because the actions of all participants are already recorded in the log file. But these actions are not always informative; for example, it may not be possible to deduce someone's real bargaining position from her actual bargaining behavior

Incentive provision is, in most cases, a more realistic strategy. There are many methods to control moral hazard through the provision of incentives. The insurance market is again a good source of examples. Co-insurance is such a strategy. For example, in most comprehensive car insurance policies in the United Kingdom, the owners are required to pay around $150 every time they make a claim from their insurance company. [5] This sum is sufficiently high to ensure that most people take precautions. But it comes at a cost: those who have taken the appropriate precautions but still need to make a claim are effectively worse off. Moreover, co-insurance may drive out of the market some people (for example, those who are on a very low risk group, say because they do not drive very much, or those who are not too averse to risk) who otherwise would have taken out an insurance policy (except of course in those countries where insurance is compulsory).

This inefficiency is not unique to co-insurance. Most strategies involving incentives have some disadvantages. Making the outcome of every agent completely dependent on his behavior (for example pricing that increases directly with the amount of insurance required) will provide participants with incentives not to consume too much insurance, but will also penalize those who really require high quantities.

In general, mixed or balanced incentives protocols tend to work best. For example, in employment contracts a fixed salary plus performance-related bonus option works very well in most circumstances. This is as true for people working on production lines as for salespeople and senior management, where it is nowadays common to include share options in the salary package. Since the options are worth more if the company is successful, the managers have an incentive to perform well. This bonus is usually given in addition to a reasonable salary, so as not to make the salary too random.

---

[5] Interestingly, this $150 payment is waived if the car is stolen from its owner's locked garage. This emphasizes the idea that this payment is designed to deter moral hazard—there is nothing the owner can do about her car being stolen from a locked garage.

The same principles apply to the design of e-commerce applications. The protocol can be designed to provide participants with incentives to achieve some measurable goal, say, the number of bits sent per unit of time over a part of the network. One way to do that is to reward the agent (financially or otherwise) in proportion to this number. This will work well as long as the agent's performance depends only on her own efforts. But if this number depends on things outside her control (for example on congestion, or if the data they are sending arrives from a different source, say their customers, at a rate that they cannot control), such a scheme will penalize agents even if their own performance is good. In the long run, it may deter organizations from using the protocol. Therefore a more balanced reward scheme will be more appropriate in such circumstances. The right balance of incentives and rewards will of course depend on the specific circumstances and can be determined only at the design stage, in consultation with potential users.

Outside options and reputation

If the same people participate repeatedly in the same protocol, then this needs to be taken into account by the designer. In some cases, simply making them better off than they would be elsewhere can be sufficient to elicit the required behaviors. Allowing participants to acquire reputations (as is done, for example, by eBay) can also improve the overall efficiency of the application.

Incentive provision needs to consider other long-term effects, such as the possibility that participants will switch between e-commerce applications (for example to trade elsewhere). In reality, the behavior of participants in one e-commerce application is likely to depend on their other options. Taking these outside options into account, the designer has an additional tool with which to elicit "desirable" behaviors. Economic analysis offers a useful way to think about this issue.

Suppose that a participant follows the designer's goals (for example, truthfully reporting her real bandwidth demand). Let w denote her benefit from this and w' her highest outside option, set to take account of losses from switching costs, such as delays and registration costs. [6] The difference $w-w'$ is known as the participant's *economic rent*, the excess earning she makes in this application compared with what she could achieve elsewhere.

Let g denote the benefit to the participant from following her own goals (which we assume are different from those of the protocol designer), where $g>w$; and let p denote the probability with which the protocol detects that participants do not follow their prescribed strategy (for example, the probability with which the protocol detects that bandwidth is consumed excessively). Let N express the length of time the participant expects to take part (in most cases, agents are likely to participate repeatedly in the protocol, for example to trade bandwidth on a daily basis). Then the participant will not follow the designer's prescribed behavior if $g>p(w-w')\cdot N$.

The incentives to not follow the designer's prescribed behavior decrease when the right-hand side of the above equation increases. The right-hand side can increase in any of the following three ways:

1. if p becomes larger, say if the protocol increases the intensity of its monitoring of behavior;
2. if N increases, that is, the participant plans to take part over a longer period;
3. if the participant's economic rent $(w-w')$ increases.

In other words, the protocol designer can elicit desirable behavior simply by making the participant better off than she would be elsewhere. This is in many cases a much simpler approach than incentive design. If participants can see benefits from long-term participation in a given e-commerce application (compared with what they can expect elsewhere), then they are much more likely to cooperate with the designer's goals.

A further implication of long-term relationships between participants and protocol (for example between traders and the marketplace where they trade) is the possibility of the former establishing *reputations*. A reputation is a highly-valued commodity in business, since it is hard to build and maintain, but very easy to lose. Someone who gained himself a reputation (for example as being truthful, say in the demands he is making or in his bargaining behavior) does not need to be monitored, or to be provided with further incentives. It is important, however, that whatever the protocol defines as a reputation is hard to

---

6   If there is some uncertainty over the possibility of being able to use the outside option (perhaps the marketplace has limited capacity), then this should make w' smaller.

obtain and easy to lose. [7] For example, the protocol can reward regular users who always pay or deliver on time by providing them with a faster service where transactions are processed before payment or delivery is verified. The protocol can reward only those who have not delayed payment or delivery for X number of times, and the service is withdrawn immediately if the user delays once.

PUTTING THE DESIGN INTO PRACTICE

Since the theory of economic design is so developed, there is also the temptation to use existing designs, which have already been tried. Although this is a good idea, the *implementation* of an existing economic mechanism to an e-commerce application may in itself create problems. For example, many auctions require that bids and announcements are made publicly. A Dutch auction is one such example. In this set-up, the price drops continuously until one of the bidders accepts it.

On a distributed system where information might reach different users with some delay, this can become a problem. Suppose that someone is trying to accept the going price but his message is delayed. The price then goes down and someone else wins the auction. The "wrong" person wins the auction (that is, not the bidder with the highest willingness to pay) and the final price is below what the seller could have got.

Timing is only one example of the problems faced by those who implement trading mechanisms on the Internet. Other problems can arise from the security requirement of the participants. For example, in chapter 7 we saw that submitting one's real willingness to pay is the best strategy in a second-price sealed bid auction. But this is based on the assumption that bids are not tampered with. If the seller, for example, finds out what these real valuations are, he can then take advantage of it. Or a bidder can infer certain information from illegally observing bids of others, and revising her own bid in response. In a non-Internet auction where bidders are physically present this is less likely to be a problem, but on the web this can be very significant. Furthermore, some trading mechanisms disseminate information such as closing prices, but not the identity of traders. Once again, if this information becomes known, it can

---

[7] The theory that formally deals with constructing "reputation" mechanisms is the theory of repeated games. See any textbook on game theory (e.g. Binmore, 1992) for more details.

be exploited. In a digital market, where information can easily be transmitted, such security issues are very important.

In general, whether a given mechanism needs to be changed before it can become an e-commerce protocol, and the scale of any such changes, will not be known before one actually starts to implement the mechanism. It may very well happen that the best option is not to fix the application so that it "fits the model", but instead to fix the model, i.e. come up with a new or modified design, that corresponds better to the specific issues arising from the application. To go back to the Dutch auction protocol (where the price falls until someone accepts it), it may be easier to replace it with an equivalent sealed bid auction than to "fix" the application, say by including a synchronization component that eliminates the risk of rejected delayed bids.

However, an understanding of both the theory and the application is necessary before deciding which route to take. If incentives exist for individuals to behave in such a way that the protocol could become inefficient, it is generally possible to change some details of the protocol so that this behavior is no longer desirable for the participants.

It is also worth noting that a successful design in one context may not work in another. For example, some of the continental European auctions of radiospectrum were comparative failures because they ignored the fact that "one size doesn't fit all". What is an appropriate design for one auction may well not work in a different context. For example, when there are incumbents, it can be sensible to design auctions to create entry. In the radiospectrum auction designers could choose how many licenses to offer and how many licenses each bidder can win. In the U.K. 3G auction there were four incumbents, but five licenses were offered and each bidder could win only one. In other words, at least one license was reserved for a newcomer. Nine bidders appeared and the auction raised £22.5 billion. In comparison, the Dutch 3G auction, which was held in the same year under similar economic conditions, raised only £1.6 billion. The auction's failure to attract competition was widely held as the source of its failure to raise more money. In Holland there were five incumbents and five licenses on offer. Pre-bidding deals to bid together were allowed. Only one (weak) entrant appeared, who was bullied, and withdrew early. Taking designs "off the shelf" without testing them to see how well they fit the conditions can therefore be dangerous.

LESSONS FOR DESIGNERS OF MARKET MECHANISMS

- The mechanisms designed by economic engineers are not machines but systems of rules and incentives that govern human interactions. But they often work just as reliably as machines, both in the laboratory and in the field.
- Designers of market mechanisms could be private sector designers or policy-makers designing an auction or a public utility trading mechanism.
- There are two key issues in designing an e-commerce mechanism: to encourage individuals or organizations to participate; and then to get them to behave in the way they are supposed to.
- Problems in ensuring participation and the "right" behavior arise from the existence of private information—information asymmetries between buyers, sellers and market makers, which lead to "prior" outcomes of adverse selection and "during" outcomes of moral hazard.
- If participants can see benefits from long-term participation in a given e-commerce application (compared with what they can expect to get elsewhere), they are much more likely to cooperate with the designer's goals.
- A successful design in one context might not work in another. An understanding of the specific features and needs of the application is important before forcing an economic mechanism onto it. Taking designs "off the shelf" can be dangerous.

Chapter 6

One-to-one Trading:
Direct Negotiations in E-commerce

Direct, one-to-one negotiations between buyers and sellers are the basic building block of the market economy. In the context of e-commerce applications, they are even more significant. There are substantially more negotiations in e-commerce than in more traditional forms of commerce because it is much easier for e-commerce sellers to sell to different customers at different prices and to change their prices in response to changes in costs or demand. Similarly, buyers have more choice of where to buy.

Furthermore, advances in automated negotiation technology make negotiations possible in a considerable number of circumstances where fixed prices were traditionally the norm. For example, it is already possible for corporate buyers to use software programs to negotiate the cost of electricity with their suppliers and to switch between them in response to changes in price or demand.

This chapter describes how economic analysis of one-to-one negotiations sheds light on the appropriate design of e-commerce applications using this form of trading mechanism. Of course, designers of e-commerce applications cannot dictate to the negotiating parties how to behave. But they can try to elicit certain behaviors by properly designing the communication protocol—the "rules of the game".

The choice of protocol will typically affect the behavior of market participants. For example, participants capable of making credible "take-it-or-leave-it" offers are typically in a good bargaining position. (Paradoxically, this is because they refuse to bargain.) The protocol determines the legal actions that buyers and sellers can take at any point. Violating the protocol can sometimes be made technically impossible—for example, preventing buyers and sellers from submitting multiple-price demands—or illegal actions can be penalized via the regular legal system.

The protocol needs to be designed carefully, taking into account the fact that all market participants will be aiming to maximize the benefits they derive from the deal. So the protocol has to provide the right incentives for the traders. Furthermore, in most negotiation settings, traders can choose whether to participate or not, so the designer must also provide incentives to enter the market in the first place.

This chapter first explains what is special about one-to-one negotiations and why auctions or exchange mechanisms cannot be used in many situations. It then describes the basic economic theory from the point of view of a designer of e-commerce applications, reviewing a number of protocols and explaining when it is appropriate to use them.

One-to-one negotiation protocols need to be tailored to the specific needs of the application where the technology is going to be used. In particular, it is important to check whether participants have private information (e.g. situations when the buyer does not know the lowest price that the seller is willing to accept), and whether they are constrained by deadlines (for example, seats on a flight must be sold by the time it leaves).

The chapter concludes with two detailed examples of e-commerce applications based on economic analysis:

1. Kasbah, an experiment conducted at MIT in 1996, in which hundreds of students, staff and faculty traded simultaneously, using selling and buying software programs equipped with some degree of negotiation skills;
2. ADEPT, an "agent-based business process management" system currently used by a number of telecoms companies. The ADEPT system uses ideas from the theory of one-to-one negotiations to facilitate efficient, automated negotiations between the various departments within large organizations.

ONE-TO-ONE NEGOTIATIONS OFF- AND ONLINE

A single buyer negotiating the terms of a deal with a single seller is the most basic of market interactions. In fact, even when there are many buyers and sellers in a marketplace, it is still likely that the favored method of negotiation is one-to-one. As long as it is costly to switch between sellers (or buyers), then negotiations will essentially be one-to-one.

Switching may be costly because it is difficult to find another seller who is selling exactly the same thing. For example, in a market for computer components, a buyer may be looking for 300 units of a certain computer processor. At any given moment, there may be only one seller capable of delivering the whole 300 units. The buyer can of course combine smaller quantities from a number of sellers, but this may take some time and involve extra costs.

So as long as the goods or services sold are not entirely standardized, one-to-one bargaining between buyers and sellers will remain an important feature of commerce whether off- or online. More generally, one-to-one bargaining will remain the trading mechanism of choice in those markets where contracts cannot be, or are not, standardized.

In consumer e-commerce, several websites have been set up that enable buyers and sellers to participate in one-to-one negotiations over the Internet. One example is HaggleWare (www.haggleware.com), which uses electronic salespeople to haggle with customers over the price of a range of products.

This is pretty much like a garage sale. At such sales you may see an item you want, but not quite at the price at which it is being offered. Instead of just walking away because the price is too high, you approach the seller and offer him a few dollars less. You begin a bargaining process. Sometimes the seller accepts your offered price or makes you a counter-offer. The negotiations result in your agreeing on a price somewhere in between the two original offers. Both you and the seller are happy because you managed to buy the item you wanted and the seller managed to sell it at an acceptable price.

HaggleWare works in exactly the same way. Once you enter the site and find a product you want to buy, you begin negotiating the price with the seller. In this case, the seller is represented by an automated negotiator. While negotiating, you have the choice of offering the seller his asking price or a price that you feel is fair. The seller can then either accept your offer, stand firm on his price or suggest another price somewhere in between. If the deal satisfies neither party, either or both can walk away from the negotiations at any time. A human element is introduced into the process by delivering characters for the negotiator and dialogue, which makes the negotiation a more personalized and engaging experience for shoppers.

Another example of a site that enables customers to haggle over the price of goods is Hagglezone (www.hagglezone.com). This site is similar to HaggleWare in that it allows real-time negotiations between the buyers and sellers of goods. It also has automated negotiators acting on behalf of the seller. The difference between the sites is that Hagglezone has a stable of hagglers from which you can choose one with which to negotiate. Each haggler has a different character and negotiating style. The different hagglers appear on screen along with a summary of their characters.

To illustrate this process, I entered into a haggle with Dot for a scooter.[1] The item was listed for $99. The negotiations went like this:

> Dot: *All right! Another haggler. How are you today? My little heart's going pitter-pat. $94.07 would put it off the Richter scale.*
> Me: *Offer $40.*
> Dot: *$80.86 will get my engines revved.*
> Me: *Offer $45.*
> Dot: *$70.42 will get us cheek to cheek.*
> Me: *Offer $50.*
> Dot: *This haggle is progressing nicely. Good work! $62.44 will make my eyelashes flutter.*
> Me: *Offer $53.*
> Dot: *Sold for $53. I want to have someone like you around if I ever need a divorce from a wealthy man.*

Notice the large difference between the original asking price and the final price. This suggests a substantial initial markup, in anticipation of negotiations. This is very similar to Middle Eastern markets where one reasonably never expects to pay the original asking price.

Automated negotiations

Automated negotiations can be used in many other e-commerce applications. For example, software programs can be used to obtain cheaper prices for utilities like basic telephone services. A simple program can be installed to monitor and direct long distance calls. The user dials the country code, and

---

[1] This took place in the summer of 2000.

as she continues to dial the telephone number the program contacts various long distance providers and negotiates the best deal for her. The program can be set up to inform the user about the price before the call is connected: for example, "The best rate for this call is 9 cents per minute with no minimum charge. If you are happy with this price and would like to continue with your call, please press 1."

Similarly, programs can be installed to monitor the consumption of household electricity. Since the software knows the pattern of electricity demand in the household, it is able to negotiate meaningfully with the various electricity providers at regular intervals. A number of experiments with this type of technology have been taking place in Scandinavia and the United States.

Automated negotiation technology can also be used to reduce negotiation overheads within large organizations. The interactions of the various departments within large organizations are often best described in terms of self-interest. Of course, they all work for the same organization, but they may be pursuing conflicting goals. The legal department may have different requirements from those of the sales department, and the technical people might impose their own constraints. Software can be used to replace much of the small-print repeated-type negotiation within the organization. These negotiations are dominantly one-to-one. (The legal department must agree with the technical department, for example, there are no outside options here.)

At the end of this chapter is a detailed description of the ADEPT system, which was designed to achieve exactly these goals, and is successfully being used by a number of telecoms companies. Along the same lines, software can be used to facilitate negotiations between individuals and organizations. The Kasbah experiment, also described at the end of this chapter, is a good example of such an application. More generally, programs that know the preferences of their users and are equipped with some degree of negotiation skills can buy, sell or schedule meetings on behalf of their users.

Finally, the Internet itself is being used as a huge marketplace for computations. The Popcorn project at the computer science department of the Hebrew University in Jerusalem (www.cs.huji.ac.il/~popcorn/) provides an infrastructure for globally distributed computation over the whole Internet. It provides any programmer connected to the Internet with a single huge virtual parallel computer composed of all processors on the Internet that care to participate at any given moment. Negotiations can take place either manually or automatically (that is, between software programs), so that owners of under-used computers can actually make money by sub letting their CPUs to those who need them.

Strategic considerations in one-to-one negotiations

In one-to-many negotiations, auctions can be used to facilitate efficient trade. Similarly, exchange mechanisms work very well in many-to-many negotiations. But neither auctions nor exchanges "scale down" to the case of one-to-one negotiations. To see why, consider the example of an auction with only one buyer. The buyer is then in the strongest possible bargaining position: any bid she submits will win the auction unless the seller specifies a reserve price, a lower limit on what prices are acceptable. In the latter case, the buyer will win only if her bid is above the reserve price, but *any* bid exceeding this price will win the auction because there is no competition. For this reason, auctions are often made conditional on at least two bidders being present. Similarly, the positive properties of exchange mechanisms, such as efficiency and transparency (which are discussed in more detail in chapter 8), are guaranteed only if there are enough participants.

In a one-to-one setting, strategic considerations become very important: players have strong incentives to manipulate their behavior in response to both the protocols and the behavior of their opponents. This is true whether or not players are privately informed.

If players have private information—for example if the seller alone knows his valuation of the goods he is selling—then the Myerson–Satterthwaite (1983) result, described in chapter 4, shows that:

- these strategic effects lead to a considerable inefficiency;
- and that this inefficiency is an inherent feature of negotiations between privately informed players.

This means that in situations where information is private it is not possible to overcome the inefficiency of negotiations by means of protocol design. And unfortunately, since private information is common in e-commerce applications, what can be achieved in terms of design is limited to start with.

Furthermore, strategic considerations affect the behavior of the bargaining parties even if there is no private information. This is because the outcomes of one-to-one negotiations are very sensitive to the details of the interaction protocol used. For example, which of the players gets to make the first or last offer can have a huge impact on who gets what. If players face strict deadlines, this too changes the outcome considerably from the case where they do not have deadlines or the deadlines are not strict. The contrast between strict and non-strict deadlines might be characterized by "I have to get my flight booked before Monday when I need to be in Chicago" as opposed to "I want to buy a book in the next three days".

This means that designers of protocols must examine carefully all the relevant features of the negotiation environment. Once again, this limits what can be achieved because every bargaining environment requires its own protocol. This is a major disadvantage of one-to-one negotiations. In one-to-many or many-to-many trading mechanisms, the problem is far less acute. Some auction structures, like the standard ascending English auction, work well in a large number of cases. Similarly, exchange mechanisms are robust to changes in the number of traders, quantities traded and other relevant features of the trading environment.

DESIGNING TECHNOLOGIES FOR ONE-TO-ONE NEGOTIATIONS

In one-to-one trading, players negotiate how to split the surplus provided by the deal—how to divide the "cake". For example, suppose that the seller will accept any price over $5 for the book he is selling. Then, if the buyer is willing to pay any price up to $10 for this book, the difference between $5 and $10 is the surplus. The number of possible splits is limited only by the units of currency, and therefore can be very large. It is actually easier to ignore the currency and think of a continuum of splits.

The surplus does not have to be money. Consider the example of two scheduling agents arranging a 15-minute meeting between their users. User A can meet any time between 3pm and 5pm but prefers to meet as early as possible, because this is her last meeting for the day. User B can meet any time between 4pm and 6pm, and would prefer to have the meeting as late as possible, because he has to be in the office for a 7pm meeting in any case. The meeting can therefore potentially take place any time between 4pm and 5pm; that is, these four 15-minute slots are the "cake" in this case. But the agents have opposite preferences over the exact time—agent A prefers the 4pm slot to the 4:15pm slot, which again she prefers to the 4:30pm slot. Her least preferred option is 4:45pm. Agent B has the exact opposite preferences, and so the two agents negotiate how to "split" their differences.

Another example is negotiating the terms of a deal. The differences in preferences here are not necessarily monetary— rather, they refer to various components of the deal. But it is still possible to think of these differences in terms of an agreement on how to "split the cake", where the "cake" is simply the set of all agreements that are acceptable to both parties.

Splitting a dollar

Economic analysis provides a way to think about any negotiation of this kind by characterizing the surplus provided by the contract as 1, and each player's fallback payoff, that is, what they would get if negotiations fail and no contract can be agreed, as 0. This simplification makes it possible to think of the huge class of one-to-one negotiation applications in terms of one simple example, "splitting-a-dollar". The conclusions from studying this single example will therefore be useful for the whole class of problems described in this chapter.

Once the protocol is set in place, a player will choose actions that maximize her own goals. If the size of the surplus is known (that is, if there is no private information), then players will choose actions that lead them to the highest possible share of the dollar. This is a somewhat cynical view of the world—in reality, people sometimes try to be "nice" in negotiations. For example, they offer their opponent a small but positive share of the cake even if they know they can get away with keeping it all to themselves. But in many cases, arguably in most business situations, this is not the case—people are not nice just to be nice. (They may be nice because they are likely to interact with the same person in the future—that is, being nice may be an investment.) In any case, it is useful to study what would happen if people are rational in the sense of goal maximization.

If players *are* privately informed, for example if the valuations of the product by the buyer and seller are known only to themselves, then the size of the cake may be unknown. Even if the size of the cake is known, it is possible that other important features, like deadlines, are private information. In this case, players' actions may also reveal their private information. For example, if the seller makes a sudden large concession, it is possible that he does so because his own deadline is approaching fast.

In this setting, players' choices of actions are more complicated. On the one hand, players still want to receive a high share of the "dollar". On the other hand, they would like to make their opponent believe that they are in a strong bargaining position. So actions are selected on the basis of both criteria. This may lead to inefficiencies. For example, players may deliberately delay agreements because they want to show that they can afford to wait, and to convince their opponent that they are in a strong bargaining position.

Simple protocols for negotiations

Economic analysis of these issues begins with the simplest case: one-to-one negotiations without private information. Consider the following simple example: two users, A and B (either real people or software programs operating on their behalf), simultaneously announce their demand for the dollar. Denote user A's demand by x and B's demand by y (where x and y are numbers between 0 and 1). The protocol then works in the following way.

- If $x+y \leq 1$, then A receives share x of the available surplus and B receives share y.
- If, $x+y<1$ then they each receive in addition half of the remaining surplus, $\frac{1}{2}(1-x-y)$.
- Otherwise A and B get nothing—negotiations fail.

To illustrate how this protocol works in practice, consider the book purchasing example from the previous section. The buyer and the seller simultaneously announce prices between $5 and $10. These announcements correspond to the x and y values in the following way: x is equal to the seller's announcement minus $5 (divided by $5, the size of the surplus, so that demands are expressed in numbers between 0 and 1); y is equal to $10 minus the buyer's announced price, once again divided by $5. If the seller's price is higher than the buyer's price, it is easy to check that $x+y>1$ and so negotiations will fail. Otherwise, they will trade at a price that is the average of the two announcements.

To determine the outcome of this protocol (assuming the players are rational), it is necessary to look at the equilibria of the game specified by these rules. Recall from chapter 2 that in equilibrium each of the players is optimizing given the behavior of the other. So, given A's demand, x, what is B's best response? Clearly, B should not ask for more than $1-x$ because he will end up with nothing. Anything less than $1-x$ means that there will be some remaining surplus. But then B will only receive half of this surplus. B's best response to A's demand of x is therefore to demand $y=1-x$. Similarly, whatever share y is demanded by B, A's best response is to demand $x=1-y$. Therefore, any pair x and y such that $x+y=1$ is an equilibrium of this simple demand game as specified by the protocol. [2]

What if the rules of the protocol are changed slightly? Suppose now that B can see A's demand, x, before making his own demand. There is no need for B to make his own demand (because there is no chance for A to respond to B's demand). So B will either accept or reject A's proposal. More formally, the protocol works as follows.

- A makes a demand x of the surplus for herself, leaving $1-x$ for player B.
- Then, B decides whether to accept A's offer. If B accepts, then A receives x share of the surplus and B receives the rest, If B rejects A's offer, then both players receive nothing and the game ends—negotiations fail.

Consider once more the book purchasing example. One of the players proposes a price between \$5 and \$10. (If it is the buyer, then x is \$10 minus their proposed price divided by \$5 and if it is the seller, then x equals his proposed price minus \$5, divided by \$5.) The other player then decides whether or not to accept this price. If she does, they trade at this price. If she does not, negotiations fail and no trade will take place.

---

2 This protocol is identical to that mentioned in chapter 4 in the context of bilateral negotiations. In chapter 4, this protocol was inefficient. The reason why the same protocol is efficient here is that there is no private information. Players know in advance the reservation price of their opponents. Since they already know it, they do not need to deduce it from observed behavior, and therefore there are no incentives to manipulate bids, as was the case in chapter 4. In the current setting, players will agree a split. But because there are so many equilibria, it is not possible to predict who will get what. All that can be said in advance is that all splits are equally likely. In reality, people use all sort of heuristics to select the outcome—for example, in most cases both players will demand one-half of the "dollar". Or if one of the players is more senior, then he is likely to agree on a split that is more in his favor.

Notice that in procedural terms not much has changed (that is, the difference between the first and second protocols *as computer codes* is very small). But it turns out that the equilibrium outcome—or the underlying incentive structure—changes considerably.

To find the equilibrium of this game, start with B's best response to A's offer. If B refuses A's offer, he gets nothing. It is therefore rational for him to accept any offer that gives him a positive share, however small. In equilibrium, A will anticipate this and therefore will offer B the smallest possible share. In other words, A will propose x very close to 1 and B will accept. There are no other equilibria.

Compare this to the first demand game, where any split was possible, and it becomes clear that, although the rule change may have been small, the change in outcomes is significant. So in this protocol it matters who gets to make the first offer (that is, who is player A). Returning once more to the book purchasing example, if the buyer is A, then she will make a take-it-or-leave-it offer of $5 to the seller, who would accept it. If the seller moves first, he will offer $10, and again, this will be accepted. The implication is that each player wants to be the one who gets to make the offer.

Alternating-offers protocols and the value of making the last offer

In most real bargaining situations, players can respond to offers by making counter-offers. Haggling is commonplace not only in Middle Eastern bazaars, but also between businesses. So how do protocols work in these types of negotiation? Begin with the previous example, where A was able to get the whole surplus by moving first. Suppose now that player B can respond to A's offer.

More specifically, A makes an initial offer of x (that is, a share x of the "dollar" to herself and $1-x$ to player B). B can either accept this offer, in which case the deal is implemented and negotiations end, or reject A's offer and make a counter-offer, i.e. share y to himself, and $1-y$ to A. Finally, A decides either to accept this offer, in which case this deal is implemented and negotiations end, or to reject, in which case negotiations fail—no one gets anything.

What is the equilibrium of this game? It is easy to see that most of the bargaining power lies now in the hands of player B, because he is making the last offer. The same logic of the previous example applies here, too: at the last stage of the game, A will accept *any* offer, and so B will offer (almost) everything to himself and A will accept (that is, *y* will be 1 or very close to 1).

This is what will happen in the second stage of the game. So what will happen in the first stage—that is, what offer will A make, and will B accept it or reject it? Clearly, any offer that gives B less than what he expects to get in the second stage will be rejected by a rational player B. So either A offers everything to B in the first stage, or her offer will be rejected.

Time discounting and bargaining power

In reality, economic actors—be they individuals, organizations or even software programs—prefer to agree sooner rather than later. In economic terms, there is a "disutility" from delaying agreements. The longer negotiations take, the more likely it is that circumstances will change—maybe the buyer will find another place to purchase the goods, or will receive a better offer. Or maybe the application will crash.

For these reasons, player B may be willing to make a small concession to A in the first stage, so that they can trade early. More formally, the "dollar" shrinks at a constant rate of δ, where δ is a positive number smaller than 1, but very close to 1. A dollar at stage 1 is worth one dollar. A dollar at stage 2 is only worth δ of a dollar. If there are more than two periods, then the dollar continues to shrink—it is only worth δ^2 at stage 3 (note that $\delta^2 < \delta$, because δ is smaller than 1), δ^3 at stage 4, and so on.

What impact does this time consideration have on the two-stage game? Player A now has gained some, small, bargaining power. She can delay the agreement to the second stage by making a "bad" offer to B—anything that gives B less than what he expects to get in the second stage. Getting the whole surplus, the whole dollar, at stage 2 is worth δ to B. So A can now offer, at the first stage, the following split: A gets $1-\delta$ and B gets δ. Since B cannot get more by rejecting this offer (that is, by moving to the second stage), he will accept. Negotiations will not continue. The game will therefore end after one period.

The logic of the two-stage alternating-offers bargaining protocol can be applied to alternating-offers protocols with more stages. Consider, for example, a five-stage alternating-offers protocol.

- Stage 0: A makes an offer.

- Stage 1: B either accepts this offer (and negotiations end), or makes a counter-offer.
- Stage 2: A either accepts this offer (and negotiations end), or makes a counter-offer.
- Stage 3: B either accepts this offer (and negotiations end), or makes a counter-offer.
- Stage 4: A either accepts this offer (and negotiations end), or negotiations fail.

In this example, B has most of the bargaining power because he is making the last offer. If the game reaches the last stage, B will get the whole surplus. But by that stage the surplus, or the dollar, will only be worth δ^4. Player A's bargaining position comes from the fact that she can make the game continue (by making bad offers to B and by refusing B's offers, except for the last one). Working backwards and assuming rationality, A will make the following initial offer to B: A gets $1 - \delta^4$ and B gets the rest, δ^4. Player B will accept this offer immediately, and the game will end after only one round.

Impatience and the outcome of alternating-offers games

What general conclusions can be drawn from this analysis? In an alternating-offers protocol, the last player to make an offer will hold most of the bargaining power, since he can expect to get the whole dollar. But the dollar will have shrunk by then. The more rounds there are, the more the dollar would have shrunk: if there are n periods of offers and counter-offers, then the dollar will be worth only δ^n by the final period.

In equilibrium, therefore, the last mover will either offer (if A is the last mover), or be offered, δ^n in the first round. The rest of the dollar, $1 - \delta^n$, will be kept by the other player. This initial offer will be accepted and negotiations will end immediately. Notice that as n grows the amount that the last mover gets— δ^n—becomes smaller. For example, if $\delta = 0.9$ and $n = 7$ then the last mover gets only 0.478 and the rest, more than one-half, goes to his opponent. So the bargaining power from making the last offer is smaller the more rounds there are.

But what if there *is no last period*? In other words, what if negotiations are allowed to continue forever, that is until the players manage to agree? This question was first addressed by Ariel Rubinstein (1982). In his analysis, negotiations could, in principle, continue forever. Rubinstein's "infinite-horizon" alternating-offers game is more complicated than any of the games presented so far, because of the richness of the set of strategies that can be used by the players. Also, because there is no last period, it is not possible to use the backward solving technique.

Rubinstein's main finding is that this game has a unique equilibrium[3] where player A makes an offer, which is then immediately accepted by B. This offer divides the dollar proportionally according to how impatient the players are, that is, to their δ values. If both players are equally impatient (that is, if both have the same δ value), then A's proposal is that the dollar be split in the following way: A will get $1/(1+\delta)$ and B will get the rest of the dollar, which is equal to $\delta/(1+\delta)$. Notice that B's share of the dollar is slightly smaller than A's (but the closer δ is to 1, the smaller this difference becomes). So there is a small advantage from being the first mover in this game. If one of the players is more impatient than the other, then the share (in equilibrium) shrinks proportionally to their degree of extra impatience.[4]

To summarize the discussion of alternating offer games: in all these games, there is a unique solution where players agree on a split immediately. This is efficient because there is no delay. This makes such games attractive as the basis for one-to-one negotiation technologies. If the game has a last period, then the person who makes that last offer can reasonably expect to obtain the whole surplus at that stage. But the later this last period is, the less bargaining power they have.

The other player's bargaining power arises from the fact that they can delay negotiations until the last period. In equilibrium, this will be anticipated and the players will agree a split at the

---

3 Formally, a unique subgame-perfect equilibrium (SPE). A SPE is a refinement of Nash equilibrium (that is, any SBE is also a Nash equilibrium, but not vice versa). SPE requires not only that players best-respond to each other, but that they do at any point of the game, i.e. regardless of the course of the game up to that point. If players choose actions once and for all, then the Nash equilibrium is a sufficient solution. However, if the game is played in stages, then the SPE is the appropriate solution concept. In alternating-offers games players move in turns and we therefore use the SPE. See Osborn and Rubinstein (1998) for more details.

4 Formally, denote by δ_A the rate at which player A's dollar shrinks in each period. Similarly, denote by δ_B player B's rate. Then Rubinstein shows that, in equilibrium, player A will receive a share $(1-\delta_2)/(1-\delta_1\delta_2)$ of the dollar, while player B receives the rest, i.e. $\delta_2[(1-\delta_1)/(1-\delta_1\delta_2)]$.

beginning of negotiation based on these two factors, that is, who the last mover is, and how long is it before the last period.

If the game can continue in principle forever, then the players' bargaining powers arise from their relative impatience. In addition there is a small advantage from making the first offer (that is, from being player A rather than B).

THE IMPORTANCE OF CONTEXT-SPECIFIC DESIGN FOR E-COMMERCE

The infinite-horizon alternating-offers game is a good example of how game theory can be used to design efficient e-commerce applications. The protocol specifies a game that is similar to real-world bargaining, and the outcome is efficient and immediate. But there are two problems that need to be addressed before this protocol can be used for one-to-one negotiations in e-commerce.

- First, the infinite horizon assumption is often not realistic. Most e-commerce applications simply cannot allow for negotiations to continue forever. Of course, if the players know that negotiations will end after a fixed number of rounds, then the outcome changes considerably.
- Second, the assumption of perfect information is also limiting. In practice, in most e-commerce scenarios participants have private information. In such settings, the infinite-horizon alternating-offers model leads to multiple equilibria, including some where agreements are made only after long delays, or never. [5]

The usefulness of these models as blueprints for designing protocols is questionable when they allow for such qualitatively different outcomes. Nevertheless, they provide an important starting point. The tools of game theory can be used to study new types of bargaining model, inspired by the various applications of automated negotiation.

A good example of this is bargaining with deadlines. In many e-commerce applications, participants must reach an agreement by a given deadline, which is private information. For example, in the ADEPT system described at the end of this chapter, software programs negotiate for services that must be

---

[5] The analysis of the infinite-horizon alternating-offers game with private information is quite complex. The interested reader can find out more by looking at Osborn and Rubinstein's textbook *A Course in Game Theory* (1998).

supplied and used by a certain time. In ADEPT, as in many similar applications, it is deadlines and not time discounting, i.e. the δ values that are the main determinant of the player's bargaining power.

Another example where deadlines are dominant is the negotiation between an airline and a potential customer for the price of the one remaining ticket on a particular flight. The plane will leave at some stage, at which time the empty seat can no longer be sold—the surplus disappears. Similarly, the customer may need to arrive at her destination at a certain time. Only the airline knows when the option of selling this ticket elsewhere is no longer viable. Similarly, the customer knows when the other flights leave and has no alternative but to buy the remaining ticket on the flight in question. For example, when a user delegates Priceline to find an inexpensive airline flight on the web, the user gives the software an hour to complete a deal. [6]

The existence of deadlines is not something that can be dealt with in any of the negotiation protocols described so far. It requires an understanding of the underlying strategic structure (that is, the game specified by these constraints and its equilibrium). Once this is understood, it is possible to design technologies for these interactions that can guarantee efficient execution of these negotiations. This is also appealing from a practical perspective, since users easily understand deadlines and can easily communicate them to software programs acting on their behalf. Hence, such technology can be used to facilitate automated interactions in a large number of e-commerce settings.

Negotiations with deadlines

A research paper by Tuomas Sandholm and Nir Vulkan (2000) studies negotiations between privately informed players who face deadlines. In this framework, each of two players faces a firm deadline. Each knows their own deadline, but not the deadline of their opponent. Each can make and accept offers at any stage of the negotiations. The payoff for a player from an agreement made *before* his deadline is his share of the dollar. If the agreement is delayed—but as long as the delay is not so long that the player misses his deadline—then the dollar

---

6 While priceline.com uses an agent with a deadline, the setting takes the form of auction, not bargaining.

shrinks at a constant rate. The payoff for a player from any agreement that takes place *after his deadline* is 0. Furthermore, a player strictly prefers to hand over the whole surplus than to miss his deadline. In other words, it is better to give the whole surplus to your opponent than to miss the deadline. This last assumption captures the essence of deadlines.

In this framework, a player's choice of action is influenced by two factors.

1. Each player wants to get as large a share as possible of the dollar.
2. But since deadlines are private information, any offer can reveal some information about the player making it. Specifically, there is a disadvantage in making offers that are rejected.

Any offer—with the exception of demanding everything—reveals some information about the proposer's deadline, namely that it cannot be very distant. (That is, any concession can be rationally interpreted as a sign of weakness of the person making it.) If the deadline were distant, the proposer would stand a good chance of being able to "out-wait" the opponent, and therefore would ask for a bigger portion of the surplus than she did. Similarly, the player making the offer would know that he offered too much if his offer is accepted: he could have done better by out-waiting his opponent.

Sandholm and Vulkan show that there is a unique equilibrium to the game specified by the deadline bargaining protocol. In this equilibrium, players do not agree to a split until the first deadline, at which time the player with the later deadline receives the whole surplus. This is a negative result, because it is not possible for players to make any sort of an agreement before their deadline.

To illustrate this result, imagine that you are a player, and that your deadline is approaching fast. You receive a very attractive offer—say your opponent is offering you 90 percent of the surplus. Sandholm and Vulkan's result states that you will refuse this offer. The intuition for this is that, using this offer, you can update your beliefs about when your opponent's deadline is. If she is offering so much, then her deadline must be very near—in fact, nearer than yours. But if you believe that her deadline is closer than yours, you will be better off refusing this offer because soon her deadline will arrive and you can get the whole surplus.

A protocol for bargaining with deadlines

Once the underlying strategic structure of deadline bargaining is understood, it is possible to design protocols that provide the right incentives for the players. Sandholm and Vulkan suggest the following mechanism, which implements the equilibrium of the deadline bargaining game.

- First, players report their deadlines—possibly insincerely—to the protocol.
- Then the protocol assigns the whole dollar to the player with the latest of the two reported deadlines. But the player is made to wait until the earlier reported deadline before the dollar is assigned to him. No further negotiations between the players are allowed.

Players can, if they choose to, report their deadlines insincerely to the protocol. For example, a player can pretend that her deadline is later than it really is. Although insincere reporting is not "punished" by the protocol, in fact, truth-telling is optimal for both players. Clearly, a player has nothing to gain by reporting that her deadline is closer than it really is. Such a report will reduce the probability of winning, and cannot therefore be optimal.

Reporting a later deadline may seem like a good idea at first glance. But it turns out that this is not optimal either. Suppose that the real deadline for player A is in 5 minutes. Can player A gain by reporting a higher value, say 10 minutes? It is useful to differentiate between two cases.

1. Player B reports a deadline of less than 5 minutes.
2. Player B reports a deadline of more than 5 minutes, for example 7 minutes.

In the first case, reporting 10 minutes instead of 5 does not matter: player A would win either way. In the second case, however, according to the rules of the protocol, player A is assigned the whole surplus after 7 minutes. But since her real deadline is 5 minutes, this is very bad for her because she will miss her deadline. In other words, player A does not want to "win" in this case. Reporting the true deadline to the protocol is therefore the (only) optimal strategy.

In fact, truth-telling is optimal regardless of what the other player does. This type of optimal strategy is known as a *dominant strategy*. Since the protocol relies on dominant strategies, it is efficient in several important ways.

- It minimizes counter-speculation. Normally, each player's best strategy will depend on what his opponent does. This requires speculation about the opponent's strategies, e.g. by considering factors such as his deadline, how rational he is likely to be, what he is likely to think about what I am going to do, etc. But in a dominant strategy mechanism, a player's strategy is optimal no matter what others do. Therefore, counter-speculation is not useful, and the player need not waste time on it.
- If software programs negotiate on behalf of agents, then there is an additional benefit in that it is easier to implement a program that executes a given dominant strategy than one that counter-speculates.
- Finally, the suggested protocol is efficient in that it minimizes communication: each player sends only one message. In other words, the potentially cumbersome process of negotiations is replaced with a simple, auction-type protocol where, instead of negotiating, players simply submit bids.

But there are also inefficiencies in the protocol, since the assignment of the dollar (i.e. the execution of the deal) is delayed until the first deadline. Since there is "disutility" from such delays (to both players), the outcome is inefficient. Can this inefficiency be fixed? Can players somehow be made (via the rules of the protocol) to agree immediately?

Why no other deadline bargaining protocols can work
A protocol that forces a 50:50 split up front will be efficient in all respects discussed above. But it turns out that these types of 50:50 protocols raise problems at an earlier stage—the stage where players decide whether to *participate* in the protocol. In most e-commerce applications of such protocols, players can choose whether or not to use the protocol. Consider the payoff from *not* participating and instead using free-form bargaining. In this case players will not be able to agree until the earlier deadline, at which time the whole surplus will be given to the player who can wait, i.e. the player with the later deadline. At the start of negotiation each player, knowing her own deadline, is able to compute the likelihood that her opponent's deadline is before (or after) her own. For example, if a player thinks the chance that her deadline is the latest at 75 percent, then she

expects to "win" the deadline bargaining game (that is, to have their opponent concede the whole surplus to her) with probability 0.75. In this fashion, each player can compute in advance, and, given her own deadline, the probability that she will get the whole surplus at some stage of the negotiation.

Suppose now that the "50:50 protocol" is introduced. Clearly, all players who believe that they can win the free-form bargaining with probability higher than $\frac{1}{2}$ (that is, all players with deadlines later than the average deadline) will choose not to participate in this protocol. But if only players with deadlines below the average participate, players with deadlines between half the average and the average (that is, those who originally thought the probability of their winning was between $\frac{1}{4}$ and $\frac{1}{2}$) should not participate. This is because their probability of winning, given that no one with a deadline higher than the average is present, is now more than $\frac{1}{2}$, so they can do better in free-form bargaining. Next, players who believed their deadlines were close to $\frac{1}{2}$ of the average would not participate; and so on. In equilibrium, no player would participate.

This argument works not only for the 50:50 split. The same argument will hold for *any* split forced in advance. The (inefficient) protocol suggested by Sandholm and Vulkan is therefore the best possible protocol for one-to-one negotiation with deadlines. This result is therefore along the same lines of the Myerson–Satterthwaite (1983) result, presented in chapter 4: it provides an upper limit on the degree of efficiency that can be achieved by any negotiation protocol in the presence of private information.[7]

THE LIMITS OF PROTOCOL DESIGN FOR ONE-TO-ONE NEGOTIATIONS

One-to-one negotiations lie at the heart of many e-commerce applications. Designing efficient protocols that facilitate such negotiations can thus have a major impact on the development of e-commerce. In particular, such protocols can be used for automated negotiations, opening the floodgate for a huge number of applications that benefit consumers and providers of services, such as electricity and telecoms.

Economic analysis of one-to-one negotiations suggests that what can be achieved by means of protocol design is limited,

[7] The difference being that in Myerson and Satterthwaite's story players are uncertain about the size of the "cake", while here the size of the cake is known, but there is uncertainty over when the cake will disappear.

and in some cases very limited: if negotiations take place between privately informed agents, then the outcome will always be inefficient. Nevertheless, proper context-specific design, such as the deadline bargaining protocol, can keep this inefficiency to a minimum.

But even if there is no private information, the protocol must be sensitive to specific features of the negotiation environment. This again limits what can be achieved by designing protocols. For example, in alternating-offers protocols, economic analysis indicates that it is of great significance who gets to make the first and last offers. Since alternating-offers protocols are widely used in e-commerce (for example in Hagglezone, Kasbah and ADEPT), these findings are very important.

In particular, if negotiations take place between automated software programs, then millions of rounds of offers and counter-offers can take place within a couple of seconds. The role of δ is therefore limited—the cake will not shrink by that much in one or two seconds—and what really matters is which program can make the last offer. The program making the last offer will refuse any offer that gives its user less than the whole surplus. If the protocol does not specify roles (that is, if in principle any of the players can be the last mover), then this is inefficient. The real bargaining will take place outside the rules of the protocol to determine which of the participating parties gets to be the player with the bargaining power.

This sensitivity of design is in sharp contrast to one-to-many and many-to-many negotiations. Most auctions and market designs can cope with some changes in the negotiation environment. For example, most new bidders can join while others leave. More importantly, the positive economic properties of auctions and markets, such as revenue maximization, economic efficiency and transparency, are to a large degree independent of the exact mechanism used. This gives the designer more degrees of freedom with which to work. Unfortunately, this is not the case in one-to-one negotiations, and the protocol designer will need to examine carefully all the relevant features of the negotiation environment before embarking on the task.

The implications for e-commerce applications

So what are the most important features of one-to-one negotiations? It is important first to understand what is the source of the players' bargaining powers.

- A player who is in a position to make a take-it-or-leave-it offer has bargaining power. Furthermore, even if the offer happens only at some future stage of negotiation, as long as it is anticipated, the player who makes this offer has bargaining power.
- A second source of bargaining power arises from impatience. The more impatient a player is, the bigger the concession he will be willing to make in order to agree the deal as soon as possible.
- Finally, when players are privately informed they may try to pretend to be in a better bargaining position than they really are. Their optimal choice of bargaining strategies will therefore be influenced by this factor. In particular, concessions made in such a setting have the disadvantage of signalling that the player may be in a weak bargaining position.

All of these factors need to be taken into account when designing the negotiation protocol. Furthermore, the designer needs to take into account the following features of the negotiation environment.

1. What exactly is being negotiated; what is the surplus over which the players bargain? Is the size of the cake, or surplus, known to both players in advance? Do players face deadlines, and are these deadlines strict?
2. What are the players' outside options? In particular, can players engage in free-form bargaining with each other, rather than using the protocol?

Once all these features are understood, it is possible to design the protocol along the following lines.

- The protocol should be as efficient as possible; for example, it should provide players with the right incentives to agree sooner rather than later.
- It should be made simple, so that players can easily find out what their optimal bargaining strategies are.
- It should minimize counter-speculation and communications.
- The equilibrium outcome should be at least as good as the players might achieve using their outside options; in other words, it should provide players with the right incentives to participate in the e-commerce application.

- It should use dominant strategy protocols whenever possible.

NEGOTIATIONS: E-COMMERCE IN PRACTICE

Two good examples of e-commerce applications of one-to-one negotiation technologies are Kasbah, an MIT experiment from 1996, and ADEPT, an automated system for inter- and intra-business trading. Both applications try to incorporate ideas from the economic analysis of one-to-one negotiations to facilitate efficient and reliable execution of the system while allowing automated software programs to be truly self-interested.

In both cases, the negotiation protocol used is essentially the alternating-offers protocol. This may be due to the fact that users are familiar and therefore comfortable with this form of negotiation. In most cases, automated software programs are privately informed. (For example, they alone know their user's willingness to pay.) Negotiation strategies are therefore designed not only to achieve the best deal, but also to deduce the others' private information from their behavior.

Kasbah

According to Chavez and Maes (1996), the aim of Kasbah was to create a virtual marketplace on the Internet where users could go to buy and sell. This was done by creating buying and selling agents that interact in the marketplace. The idea behind it was to help users with the process of buying and selling products, particularly with the process of negotiating with other buyers and sellers. This was done by providing agents that could independently negotiate in order to make the best possible deal on their users' behalf.

Selling agents

A selling agent can be thought of as being analogous to a classified advertisement. When a user creates a selling agent he gives it a description of the product he wants it to sell. Unlike classified ads though, the selling agents are not passive and do not sit around waiting for people to respond to them. Instead, Kasbah agents are pro-active and go into the marketplace to try to sell themselves. They contact any parties (buying agents) that are possibly interested in what they have to sell and then enter into price negotiations with them with the aim of achieving the best deal they can.

The selling agents are autonomous. Once released into the marketplace, they make decisions independently without requiring interaction from the user. However, the user retains a high degree of control over the agent's behavior. When creating a new selling agent, the user sets certain parameters to guide the agent through the process of selling the product.

- *Desired date to sell the product by*: the deadline by which the user wants to sell something; for example, someone moving house may need to sell some furniture before the moving date.
- *Desired price to receive for the product*: the price that the user would ideally like to get for the product.
- *Lowest acceptable price to receive for the product*: the lowest price that the user would be willing to sell the product for. People may set the desired price at an optimistically high level in case someone is willing to buy at that level; their lowest acceptable price is set at a more realistic level.

These parameters define the agent's goal: to sell the product for the highest possible price. This would ideally be the desired price but could be as low as the lowest acceptable price if that is what it takes to be able to sell the product in the time frame set. Once the parameters are set, the agent is free to choose how to achieve this goal. This frees the user's time and energy to pursue other activities. In addition, it is likely that the agent would be more effective than a human at achieving the best possible price. This is due to its advantages of fast processing speed and communication bandwidth.

Seller negotiation strategy
Selling agents begin by offering the product at the user's desired price. If there is a buyer willing to buy it at that price, then no negotiation is necessary and the product is sold. If no buyers are interested at the desired price, the selling agent reduces the asking price over time to attract more buyers. When the deadline is reached, the asking price for the product is equal to the user's lowest acceptable price.

The user has some control over the agent's negotiation strategy in that he can specify the function the agent uses to reduce the asking price over time—he can choose between a linear, quadratic or cubic function. In addition, the user can check on the selling agent at any time. He can see which buying agents it has communicated with and also what prices it has offered and been offered. Such information is useful to the user as it could prompt him to alter his price parameters if the offers coming in are significantly below what is being asked. Finally, the user always has the final say in any negotiation process. When a selling agent reaches an agreement with a buying agent, the user can choose to approve the deal before the product is sold.

Buying agents

Buying agents are essentially the symmetric opposite of selling agents. Their goal is to buy products in the marketplace on behalf of their user. Returning to the analogy of a want ad, a buying agent can be thought of as an ad that actively searches for and buys what it is looking for.

When creating a buying agent, the user describes the item she wishes to buy. Alternatively, the user can specify a set of selling agents in the marketplace, for example just those in a particular geographical region, and direct them to buy from one of them. As with the creation of selling agents, the user specifies a set of parameters to guide the buying agent's behavior.

- *Date to buy the product by:* the deadline by which the user wants to buy the product.
- *Desired price to pay for the product:* what the user would ideally wish to pay for the product.
- *Highest acceptable price to pay for the product:* the highest price the user would be willing to pay for the product.

Once these parameters are set, the agent has its goal defined: to buy the product for the lowest possible price. It is free to go about achieving that independently of user interaction.

Buyer negotiation strategy

Buying agents begin by offering the user's desired price for the product. If there is a seller willing to sell it at that price, then no negotiation is necessary and the product is bought. If no sellers are interested at the desired price, the buying agent increases the offered price over time to attract more sellers. When the deadline is reached, the offered price for the product is equal to the user's highest acceptable price.

As with selling agents, the user has some control over the agent's negotiation strategy. She can choose the form of the agent's price-raising function from the choices linear, quadratic or cubic. The user also has the final approval for any prospective purchase and can monitor what her agent is doing at any time.

Services and benefits provided
Using agents has several advantages.

- *It spares the user from having to find and negotiate with buyers and sellers:* Kasbah basically eliminates human-to-human contact. This overcomes barriers such as those presented by language and time zone differences. It also saves the user both time and energy, which can now be used to pursue less menial tasks.
- *It lets people know who the prospective buyers and sellers are:* using agents to carry out such negotiations means that there is an accessible record of everyone they have communicated with. This can be very useful if, for example, a potential buyer asks for clarification on the product's description. Such a request may come from several potential buyers at different times. A person would respond individually to this request, which is time-consuming and annoying. In contrast, an agent can respond to such a request by pre-emptively sending the required information to all the buyers it has come into contact with.
- *It enables better pricing:* the agents record not only the other agents they have communicated with but also the communications they have had. For example, they store records in the form: "Agent 21 made an offer of $50". This enables users to gather information about the market, and means that they know if they are asking too much or are willing to pay too little for a given product. They can thus adjust their agent's parameters and achieve a better result than would probably be possible through human interaction.

The marketplace
Buying and selling agents meet and negotiate in the Kasbah marketplace. Its function is to facilitate the interaction between these agents.

The primary function required of a marketplace is to ensure that all the agents using it speak a common language. In addition, Kasbah matches up agents interested in buying or selling similar products. When agents are created, the marketplace asks them what it is they are interested in buying or selling. If it is a buying agent, the marketplace then sends it a list of all potential sellers of that product. It also sends all potential sellers a message to inform them that a new potential buyer has entered the marketplace. A similar process occurs when selling agents are created: they are given a list of all potential buyers in the marketplace, while the potential buyers are sent a message informing them that a new potential seller has entered the marketplace.

Trial run of Kasbah

The Kasbah system had two trial runs, both one-day events at MIT. A version was run in mid-October 1996 involving students, staff and faculty, and was in preparation for a later full deployment. This was held on October 30 and involved 200 people (largely from technological industries). Everyone was given books, souvenirs and play money to participate in a full-day Kasbah marketplace. Participants were encouraged to create agents to sell the items they were given and to buy items they would like. Over the course of the day, more than 250 transactions were made—a large number, given the number of participants. The experiment yielded useful insights into the use of software agents to trade on behalf of their users and also into the use of virtual marketplaces to match buyers and sellers of similar goods.

ADEPT

Companies have traditionally had fairly centralized structures, but this is becoming less common in the face of globalization, technology and the flattening of traditional management structures. Organizations are becoming more "distributed"—made up of a number of individual units that may be diverse in both geography and the way they work.

Management of such diverse business units is a complex operation, implying the need for decisions based on a combination of judgment and information from many different departments. The ideal situation would be to have all the relevant information brought together before judgment is used. But obtaining up-to-date information across a large company is a complex and time-consuming process. This is why many companies have sought to develop information technology systems to assist with various aspects of the management of their business processes.

ADEPT is just such a system, designed to aid the management process. It combines the latest distributed computing techniques with the technology of autonomous software programs for routine negotiations and transactions. The result is a system that can manage business processes automatically while remaining under management control. Its aim is to make inter-business and intra-business trading more effective.

The ADEPT system comprises a number of elements.

Agents

Any business process, whether carried out by people or software, is made up of a number of tasks. Since dependencies exist between these tasks, they must be carried out in a controlled and ordered way. There are several characteristics common to most business processes. Examples are the involvement of multiple organizations or departments, a high degree of task concurrency, and a need to monitor and manage the overall process.

Given these characteristics, the most natural way to view the business process is as a collection of autonomous, problem-solving agents that interact when they have interdependencies. In this context, an agent would have the following characteristics.

- *Autonomy*: agents perform the majority of their problem-solving tasks without the direct intervention of humans or other agents.
- *Social ability*: agents interact, when appropriate, with other agents in order to complete their problem-solving activities.
- *Responsiveness*: agents perceive their environment and respond to changes that occur in it.
- *Pro-activeness*: agents do not simply act in response to their environment, but take the initiative when appropriate.

In the ADEPT system, the agents represent individual departments. The functions that would traditionally be carried out by the department are carried out instead by an agent.

Services

Each agent offers services to other agents. A service is a task or package of tasks that equips an agent for some functional operation. Each service is managed by an agent. The agent offering the service is known as the service provider while the agent requesting the service is the client.

Since agents are autonomous, there are no control dependencies among them. Therefore, if an agent requires a service that is managed by another agent, it cannot simply instruct that agent to start the service. Instead, the agents must come to some form of mutually acceptable agreement about the terms and conditions under which the service will be performed. The mechanism for reaching such agreements is negotiation.

Negotiation
Agents need to interact with each other in order to achieve their objectives. This could be either because they do not have the capabilities or resources to undertake a particular action independently, or because there are interdependencies between the agents. The objective of an agent in these interactions is to make other agents undertake a particular action, i.e. perform a particular service. Since the agents have no direct control over one another, this is accomplished through negotiating with other agents to try to persuade them to act in a particular way.

Just as managers of departments would negotiate, agents negotiate with each other on how they can work together to support an overall business process. The process begins with the agents making contradictory demands. They then move toward an agreement by a process of concession making. Negotiations usually involve parameters such as quality, time and cost.

Service-oriented negotiations In service-oriented negotiations, agents' objectives are in conflict. An example would be a client who wants a low price for a service where the service provider wants to obtain the highest possible price. Another would be a client wanting to ensure the highest quality for a service and the service provider wanting to provide the service at the lowest possible quality.

Once the agents have determined the set of variables over which they will negotiate, for example cost and quality, the negotiation process between them begins. This consists of the agents alternately making offers and counter-offers of values for these variables. The process continues until one agent accepts an offer or until one agent terminates the negotiation, for example because it had a time deadline that expired.

Negotiation tactics   Tactics are the set of functions that determine how to compute the value of a quantitative issue (price, volume, duration, etc.) by considering a single criterion (time, resources, previous offers, etc.).

• *Time-dependent tactics*   In these tactics, the predominant factor used to decide which value to offer next is time. Thus, these tactics entail varying the acceptance value for the issue under negotiation depending on the remaining negotiation time. As the deadline approaches for an agreement to be made, the agent makes offers converging on the reservation value.

• *Resource-dependent tactics*   These tactics are similar to time-dependent ones. The difference is that, whereas time vanishes constantly up to the deadline, other resources may have different patterns of usage. The scarcer the resource, the more urgent the need for an agreement to be reached.

• *Imitative tactics*   These tactics compute the next offer based on the previous behavior of the opponent. However, the type if imitation can vary. Agents can make offers based on proportionally imitating the opponent, that is, reproducing in percentage terms the behavior of the opponent. This is known as *relative tit-for-tat. Random absolute tit-for-tat* is similar but here the agent imitates in absolute terms. For example, if an agent decreases its offer by $2 then the opponent's response would be to raise its offer by $2. The final form of imitation is *averaged tit-for-tat.* Here the agent computes the average of percentage changes in its opponents offer history when determining its new offer.

   To illustrate the concept of imitative tactics, here is an example of an issue for which the value is under negotiation. A client with a range [$0, $20] for the price to pay for a product may start the negotiation process by offering the server $10. The server, with a range [$17, $35] may then make an initial counter-offer of $25. Given these initial values, the strategy of the first agent may consist of using a time-dependent tactic giving $12. This would be the case if it had a short time to reach an agreement and thus began conceding. If the strategy of the server agent is to use an imitative tactic, it would generate a counter-proposal of $23, that is, imitating the $2 shift of its opponent. This process would continue until an agreement was reached.

Negotiation strategies   The aim of an agent's negotiation strategy is to determine the best course of action that will result in an agreement on a contract and maximize its scoring function. In practical terms, this equates to deciding how to prepare a new counter-offer.

When an agent receives an unsatisfactory offer, it must generate a counter-offer. Different combinations of tactics can be used to generate counter-offers for particular issues. An agent's strategy determines which combination of tactics should be used at any one time.

Given that agents may wish to consider more than one criterion to compute the value of a single issue, the counter-proposals are generated as a weighted combination of different tactics covering the set of criteria. The values computed for the different issues will be the elements of the counter-proposal. For example, if an agent wants to counter-propose taking into account two criteria—the remaining time and the previous behavior of the opponents—it can select two tactics: a time-dependent tactic and an imitative tactic. Each of the selected tactics will suggest a value to counter-propose for the issue under negotiation. The actual value that is counter-proposed will be the weighted combination of the two suggested values.

An example of when this weighted combination may be useful is when modeling a smooth transition from behavior based on a single tactic (when the agent has plenty of time to reach an agreement) to one based also on time (when the time to reach an agreement is running out). Smoothness is obtained by progressively changing the weight affecting the tactics.

An example of agents at work   Consider the departments of a business that need to work together with the sales department. The agent representing the sales department might negotiate with the other agents for services relating to the sales function. This could involve negotiating for manufacturing capacity from one agent and for delivery services from another agent. These agents may in turn require services from other departments. For example the agent providing manufacturing services may need supplies from stores for which it must negotiate with the agent representing stores. As these negotiations proceed, agreements are reached and contracts are struck.

Application to British Telecom
To provide a detailed context for this work, a multi-agent system for managing a British Telecom (BT) business process is

presented. This is an example of service-oriented negotiation between agents. This scenario is based on BT's business process of providing quotations for designing a network to provide particular services to a customer.

The overall process receives a customer service request as its input. As its output, it generates a quote specifying how much it would cost to build a network to realize the requested service. The process involves up to six agents, including agents for the sales department, the customer service division, the legal department, the design division, the surveyor department and the various agents that provide the outsourced service of vetting customers.

The process is initiated when the sales agent negotiates with the consumer service department (CSD) agent for the service of providing a customer quote. These negotiations are mainly over time but also over the form in which the final result should be delivered.

The first stage in the process of providing a customer quote involves the CSD agent ensuring that the customer is creditworthy. This vetting of a customer's creditworthiness is actually performed by one of the vetting consumers (VC) agents— representing the external enterprises which may provide the outsourced activity of vetting the customer. The CSD agent must therefore negotiate with the VC agents to determine which of them should perform the service. These negotiations mainly involve the price of the service, the desired quality of the service and the time by which the service should be performed. If the customer fails the vetting procedure, the process terminates.

Assuming that the customer passes, the CSD agent maps its requirements against a service portfolio. If the requirements can be met by an off-the-shelf portfolio item, then an immediate quote can be offered.

In the case of bespoke services, however, the process is more complex. The CSD agent must negotiate (over time and quality) with the design division (DD) agent for the service of designing and costing the desired network service. In order for the DD agent to provide this service, it must in turn negotiate with the legal department (LD) agent (over time) and perhaps with the service division (SD) agent. The LD agent checks the design to ensure the legality of the proposed service. If the desired service is legal, then the design phase of the process can start.

To prepare a network design, it is usually necessary to have a detailed plan of the customer's existing equipment. If the customer site needs to be surveyed to retrieve such information, the DD agent must negotiate with the SD agent (over price and time) for the survey service.

On completion of the network design and costing, the DD agent informs the CSD agent, which informs the customer of the service quote. The business process is then terminated.

Lessons from Kasbah and ADEPT

- Automated one-to-one negotiation technology can be used in e-commerce interactions within large organizations (as in ADEPT), between organizations (ADEPT) and between individuals (Kasbah).
- The technology can overcome problems of language, time zones and whatever other barriers there may be to human negotiations.
- Data from automated negotiations (such as log files containing all the offers) can be used to analyze and improve the design of the software programs, acting for the users, and of the communication protocol.
- The communication protocols used in Kasbah and ADEPT were based on alternating-offers.
- The negotiating agents used in Kasbah and ADEPT were based on retaliatory concession rates.
- Alternating-offers protocols and concession rate strategies resemble human bargaining behavior and are therefore easy for users to comprehend and get used to.

- More efficient protocols can be designed, based on game-theoretical principles and an understanding of the negotiating environment. Such protocols can eliminate much of the inefficiency associated with human bargaining.

KEY CONSIDERATIONS FOR E-COMMERCE NEGOTIATIONS
What designers need to think about

The key issues are:

- private information;
- deadlines;
- who goes last.

The key features of the negotiation environment are:

- what exactly is being negotiated;
- whether size of the surplus is known to both players in advance;
- whether there are deadlines and how strict they are;
- the players' outside options.

The protocol should:

- be as efficient as possible, providing players with the right incentives to agree sooner rather than later;
- be as simple as possible, so that players can easily find out what their optimal bargaining strategies are;
- minimize counter-speculation and communications;
- provide an equilibrium outcome at least as good as the players can achieve using their outside options—in other words, provide players with right incentives to participate in the e-commerce application;
- use dominant strategy protocols whenever possible.

What market participants need to know

Market participants need to know the sources of players' bargaining powers.

- A player who is in a position to make a take-it-or-leave-it offer has bargaining power.
- A second source of bargaining power arises from impatience: the more impatient a player is, the larger the concession he will be willing to make in order to agree the deal as soon as possible.
- Finally, when players are privately informed, they may try to pretend to be in a better bargaining position than they really are. Their optimal choice of bargaining strategies will therefore be influenced by this factor. In particular, making concessions in such a setting has the disadvantage of signalling that the player may be in a weak bargaining position.

Chapter 7

One-to-many Trading:
Online Auctions

Auctions are among the oldest of economic institutions, dating from at least as far back as Roman and Babylonian times. Most famously, the whole Roman Empire was sold at an auction in AD 193 by the Praetorian Guards (see Gibbon, 1776). A huge amount of trade takes place through auctions: it is, for example, the dominant method for selling art and wine, as well as being widely used for procurement for governments and large organizations.

The Internet has become a popular medium for carrying out auctions for just about all types of goods and services. Online auctions account for large part of e-commerce transactions. It is difficult to measure such a fast growing market, but even the most conservative estimates are huge. Jupiter Communications, for example, estimates that consumer-to-consumer (C2C) auctions will account for more than $5 billion by 2004, and that business-to-business (B2B) auctions already account for $10 billion and will increase to $15 billion by 2004. Hundreds of thousands of different auctions take place every day on the Internet, and a large proportion of Internet users have participated in an auction at some stage.

This chapter reviews the major differences between off- and online auctions, classifying the different types of mechanism that can be used in either context, as well as the different types of goods and services put up for auction and the different types of online auction.

The chapter then describes how economic analysis of this trading mechanism—the subset of game theory known as auction theory—sheds light on the appropriate design of auctions. In particular, it focuses on more important auction formats and their properties: optimal bidding strategies and equilibrium outcomes. Significant theoretical results from economic analysis of auctions, such as the revenue equivalence theorem, are very useful in the context of e-commerce. But because the theory is extensive, the chapter reviews only some of the more important results. Readers who are interested in finding out more about the fast-growing literature on auctions are referred to one of the many reviews, notably that by Paul Klemperer (1999).

By far the most common auction format used on the web is the English auction. The chapter reviews this type of auction and how it can work on the web. A central issue is the need for a closing date in an online auction, which results in a great deal of late bidding. There are a number of problems that can be caused by late bidding, and the chapter reviews the evidence on how successful online auction designs are in addressing these problems.

There is also a discussion of further issues that are unique to Internet auctions and the challenges and opportunities that arise from them. In particular, I describe the decision support tools designed to assist corporate purchasers participating in a number of simultaneous online auctions.

Readers of this chapter should find information on how to design a web-based auction and how to bid in one. The chapter also contains useful information on how to avoid pitfalls and possible abuses. It concludes with a summary of new issues arising from e-commerce auctions.

TYPES OF AUCTION
There are four main types of auction:

- English auctions; [1]
- Dutch auctions, [2] so named because they were traditionally used to sell flowers in the Netherlands;
- first-price sealed bid auctions;
- second-price sealed bid auctions.

---

[1] English auctions are sometimes referred to as ascending bid auctions. This may be a bit confusing, since in a reverse English auction the prices actually descend, and so I stick with the term "English" auction.

[2] Dutch auctions are sometimes referred to as descending bid auctions.

These types of auction have evolved in various countries and industries around the world as a method of selling goods. Each has rather different properties, which have implications for their appropriateness in e-commerce.

English auctions can be forward or reverse. In a forward English auction, the price rises continuously, raised either by an auctioneer (which could be a computer program) or by the bidders themselves, until there is only one buyer willing to pay the announced price. The bidder then wins the auction and pays this price. In a reverse (or procurement) English auction, it is the buyer who is the auctioneer and the price drops until there is only one seller left bidding. Bidders can observe who quits the auction and at what price. Once bidders quit the auction, they are not allowed to get back into it.

In a *Dutch auction*, the seller is once again the auctioneer and the price drops until one of the bidders accepts the going price. In the Dutch flower market, for example, there is a large clock denoting the current price, which moves continuously until one of the buyers, all of whom can observe the clock, presses his button to indicate that he is willing to buy at the current price. This bidder then wins the auction at this price.

Unlike the English auction, bidding strategies used in the Dutch auction cannot be observed, because only one bid is placed before the auction closes. A Dutch auction is not unlike some end-of-season sales, where the price of certain goods is reduced initially by a certain amount, reduced further after a fixed period of time, and then again and again until everything is sold.

English and Dutch auctions typically take place with all bidders physically present; even if bidders are not physically present, traditional auction houses such as Sotheby's require that a bidder keep in constant telephone link with the auction. This is because in both auctions, bidders need to see and respond to changes in the price.

An alternative approach is to conduct a sealed bid auction. Governments and large organizations traditionally use sealed bid auctions to sell used cars, possibly because these are more appropriate for auctions running over a few days and time zones. In this type of auction, bidders submit their bids, by post, fax or e-mail, to the seller (or to an auctioneer). Once bids are submitted, they are considered final.

In a *forward first-price sealed bid auction*, the winner is the bidder with the highest bid who is liable to pay her bid. Similarly, in a reverse first-price sealed bid auction, the bidder with the lowest bid wins the auction and is liable to sell the product or service at this price.

In a *forward second-price sealed bid auction* (also known as a Vickrey auction, after the late Nobel Laureate for Economics, William Vickrey), the winner is still the bidder with the highest bid but this time she is only liable to pay the second highest price. Similarly, in a reverse Vickrey auction, the winner is the supplier with the lowest price, who then is liable to supply the product or service at the second lowest price. This type of auction has been used to sell stamps for many years. While these auctions may initially seem less "natural", they have some useful theoretical properties, and it is likely that the realization of these properties led people to use them in the first place.

In addition to selecting the auction format, the seller can reserve the right to sell the object to the highest bidder only if this bid is above a certain reserve price. Similarly, in a reverse auction, the buyer can accept the outcome of the auction only if the price is below her reserve price. Reserve prices can be used in all the main four types of auction.

Which of these auction formats to choose is an interesting question that is addressed throughout this chapter. There is no one simple answer, because which design is most appropriate will depend on how participants respond to it, and that is something that cannot be predicted with accuracy. Nevertheless, some features of the trading environment correspond better to one particular auction type than to others.

What is being auctioned?

Auctions can also be classified according to the value of the good or service being auctioned, distinguishing between:

- private value auctions;
- pure common value auctions;
- correlated value auctions.

In a *private value auction*, the value of the product or service for each bidder does not depend on the valuation of anyone but this bidder. A meal in a restaurant and tickets for tonight's concert are both examples of private value goods. So are raw materials for manufacturers. More generally, any goods that are going to be consumed directly by the bidder fall into this category.

In contrast, the value to the bidder of owning a product that is *pure common value* is determined entirely by the how much others value it. Auctions for Treasury bills are a good example. Treasury bills have no intrinsic value to the buyer if they cannot be resold. They are essentially pieces of paper, and are worth only as much as other people are willing to pay for them.

A *correlated value auction* is somewhere in between a private value and a pure common value auction. The value of the product or service to each bidder depends partially on her own valuation and partially on how others value it. For example, the value of a painting may depend on how much an individual likes it and also on how much other people like it. Or someone may be participating in an auction to provide a service that she can either provide herself or resell. In fact, many things fall under the correlated value category. Take buying a house. The value of the house to a particular buyer depends both on how much they like it (for example, some buyers prefer a large garden to an extra bedroom), and on the market value of the house—which is essentially the common value of a property of a certain size in a certain location.

Types of online auction

Online auctions can be divided into three major categories:

1. *consumer-to-consumer (C2C) auctions*, like eBay, the world's largest online auction house, where individuals and organizations place items for sale on the auction site, which then runs the auction on their behalf for a fee;

2. *business-to-consumer (B2C) auction sites* or merchant sites, such as First Auction, uBid and Onsale, where auctions are typically used either to promote new products or to sell surplus stocks;

3. *business-to-business (B2B) auctions*, like FreeMarkets online and Moai, where companies provide the technology and run auctions for members only.

In C2C auctions, the transaction of goods and money takes place directly between sellers and auction winners. C2C sites are a modern form of a marketplace where buyers and sellers meet, and where prices are negotiated on the basis of the rules of the auction used.

B2C auction sites are similar to online stores with the only difference being that prices are not fixed. Priceline is a particularly interesting example of a B2C site, not least because it managed to patent its system. Priceline allows consumers to "name their own price" on flights, hotel accommodation and car rental. It is then left for airlines, hotels and car rental groups to decide whether to accept the best offers from Priceline customers to sell their unsold flights seats and hotel rooms and to hire cars. Interestingly, Priceline plays down the "auction" part, possibly to enhance the impression of consumers getting bargains, rather than competing to see who will pay the most for unsold flight tickets.

B2B auctions are particularly common in markets with large demand and supply fluctuations, like the markets for electronic components, and in markets for standardized goods, such as metal, steel and other raw materials.

Although all these types of auction are similar (indeed, almost all web-based auctions are English auctions), they are used for different reasons. In particular, while most B2C and B2B sites sell new goods, C2C sites are used to sell second-hand or unwanted goods. Most of the items sold on eBay for example would have otherwise ended up in the garage. Before Internet auctions became popular, some of these items would have been sold at a garage sale or through the small ads, or possibly not sold at all. Selling the item on eBay is actually cheaper than running an ad and it reaches a much larger audience. A C2C site such as eBay, which runs around 10 million different auctions every month, is the ideal place to sell since it is where most consumers will be looking.

WHY USE AUCTIONS?

Why do market participants decide to use auctions rather than alternative trading mechanisms? B2B forward auctions are typically used to maximize revenue for sellers. (Similarly, reverse or procurement auctions are used to minimize costs.) By setting a fixed price, the seller is relying on a guess as to what the buyers are willing to pay for the item sold. By running an auction, the seller is letting the buyers name their prices in a competitive setting.

A well designed auction can therefore maximize the seller's revenue. Suppose, for example, that there are five people who are interested in buying a rare painting. The best the seller could ever do is to somehow get into the heads of these five buyers, figure out how much each of them is willing to pay, and then fix the price to equal the highest of those valuations. Although such a strategy is not feasible, a well designed auction can come a pretty close second best. More specifically, by using a well designed auction, the seller can ensure that the painting is sold to the person with the highest valuation and that the price paid will be at least as high as the second-highest valuation, and possibly higher than that.

Many buyers are attracted to the game-like features of an auction, especially for low-dollar items. This is true in general, not just for auctions. When the sums involved are small, most people like to gamble, as the success of national lotteries clearly shows.

A further attraction of auctions is that they provide an effective way of resolving "one-to-many" bargaining situations. Rather than spending time and effort negotiating separately with each of the potential buyers, the auction can allocate the item to the buyer with the highest willingness to pay quickly and efficiently.

This is even more relevant for online auctions, for two reasons.

- First, fast agreements with less communication should be preferred when negotiations are carried out on the Internet, where communication can be costly and subject to frequent delays.
- Second, some of the better auction structures require bidders to compute complex strategies using automated software programs often referred to as "bidding elves".

The cost advantage of online auctions

The phenomenal success of online auctions can be explained partly by the fact that Internet technology lowers the cost of setting up and running an auction and of participating in auctions. Consumers can bid in C2C and B2C auctions without leaving their homes. And since most of these auctions run for more than a day, bidders can participate at their leisure. Sellers' costs are also low, because setting up an online auction, for example on eBay, is even cheaper than placing an ad in the newspaper. And on top of the lower cost, there is the thrill of bidding, which seems to have captured the enthusiasm of millions of consumers.

Internet technology has also lowered the costs of B2B auctions. Here auctions allow markets to respond quickly to changes in demand and supply. Although this was still true before e-commerce, the high costs of organizing an auction (for example, getting everyone to the same place at the same time) meant that they were not used very often. Similarly, the costs of continuously adjusting prices, through negotiations with suppliers, were considerably high. These costs translated into more "sticky" prices, and fewer real-time adjustments. Nowadays, companies such as Ariba, CommerceOne, Moai and FreeMarkets provide companies with the ability to conduct forward and reverse auctions at very low costs.

The reduced costs of running auctions translate into lower commissions. Sotheby's, the auction house, for example, charges buyers 15 percent and sellers 20 percent. In contrast, eBay's maximum charge is 5 percent, and this figure falls with the price of the item (down to 1.25 percent for amounts over $1,000). C2C auction sites, such as eBay, Amazon and Yahoo, also charge a fixed fee (typically between $0.50 and $2) for placing an item on their site.

Commissions on B2B auctions are also very different from those charged by traditional auction houses. Companies like Ariba and CommerceOne are essentially technology providers, in contrast with Sotheby's, which "provides the bidders"—its auctions are a meeting place and a focal point for buyers interested in fine arts. While the exact charges are different between the different auction technology providers (the charges are also different by consumer), in most cases no direct commission is charged. Instead, companies pay a license, which enables them to use the technology to run as many auctions as they want.

Automated auctions

So far, the focus has been on auctions that take place between individuals and organizations. But there are other auctions—automated auctions—where the bidders are software programs. These auctions are currently being implemented to allocate tasks and determine priorities *within* PC networks, Intranets and on the Internet.

For example, automated auctions can be used as a mechanism to determine CPU time allocation among various simultaneous computing processes. At any given time, there will be dozens of processes running on a typical PC—all of which require CPU time. Currently, PCs are installed with an algorithm determining which of these processes will be served and when. This is based on a queue and priorities.

This approach works well in the current situation, where all processes "belong" to the same PC. In the future, however, various computing devices will all be connected through the Internet or Intranets, and so the CPU of one machine may very well be used to handle computing process "belonging" to other computers. A competitive framework can therefore be adopted, for example using automated auctions whereby processes are the bidders and the CPU is the seller. Processes will bid to gain priority access to the CPU—the more urgent the process, the more it is "willing" to pay.

An auction may very well be the best mechanism to allocate the CPU time because the CPU does not know the real priorities of the incoming processes. (Users can pretend to give priority to whatever task they are doing.) By forcing users to "put their money where their mouth is", a better and fairer allocation may be obtained. Along the same lines, auctions can be used at various network bottlenecks, including the web itself, to determine priorities. For example, auctions are being used to allocate Internet traffic and bandwidth.

Auction theory applies equally whether bidders are people or pieces of software. Since the theory describes what rational bidders do (or, rather, what they should do), it can be used as the blueprint for designing software bidders. Automated auctions are suitable in places where people cannot trade, perhaps because trade takes place too quickly. For example, there could be millions of auctions to determine access to a CPU every second. Advances in auction technology now make it possible to use auctions to allocate scarce resources efficiently in a wide range of interactions.

The potential for abuse in online auctions

On the negative side, Internet auctions are more susceptible to fraud than offline auctions. The winner in an eBay auction, for example, has to send her payment to a seller she has never met before she receives the item. Fraud is potentially a very serious problem, because if the website gets a reputation for fraud, then consumers will not use it. (This is essentially the adverse selection argument discussed in chapter 5.)

In practice, however, fraud does not seem to be a significant problem on C2C sites. C2C sites allow buyers to view what previous buyers say about sellers, hence making it possible for sellers to gain reputations for honesty. For more expensive items, third-party escrow services (where the buyer sends her money to the third party, who keeps it until the buyer receives the object and only then releases the money to the seller) are frequently used, which further reduce the risk of fraud.

Along the same lines, because it is difficult to keep track of the real identity of bidders, online auctions are susceptible to various forms of strategic bidding. Sellers, for example, can use false user names to bid in their own auction, forcing potential buyers to bid more aggressively. If the seller happens to win his own auction, he can simply auction the item again.

Another form of strategic bidding is when a bidder bids twice in the same auction, placing a very low bid and a very high bid. The high bid is placed to deter other bidders from participating in the auction. But just before the auction closes, the bidder withdraws her high bid and wins the object at the low bid. Strategic bidding of this kind is not unique to online auctions, but the relative ease of carrying out such strategies on the Internet makes such behavior more of a risk for online auctions.

Fraud and strategic bidding are far less of a problem in B2B auctions, because there is normally a small number of bidders who are known either to the seller or to the technology provider and so are less likely to get away with cheating. The problems faced by B2B auction technology providers are different.

The main difficulty lies with the non-price attributes of the product or item sold, which tend to be very important in such transactions. Most business-to-business transactions depend not only on price, but also on other attributes, such as quantities available, quality assurances, guaranteed time to delivery and after-sale support. To run an auction, therefore, it is necessary first to reduce all these parameters into a single parameter, that is, price. This may not be that simple to do.

Moreover, sellers who compete to supply a corporate customer are typically better off not participating in a reverse auction, and so it is in their interest to differentiate themselves from competition through these non-price attributes. For these reasons, B2B auctions are restricted mostly to highly standardized commodities such as cement, steel and other raw manufacturing materials. Even for such commodities, vendors may still be reluctant to participate in a procurement auction that empowers the buyer. For example, they might prefer to trade via an exchange mechanism (the subject of chapter 8), which offers the same degree of flexibility in adjusting to changes in demand and supply, but does not make buyers better off at the cost of making sellers worse off.

Despite all these difficulties, auctions remain a simple yet powerful design tool, which combines flexibility—by allowing real-time price discovery and the ability to adjust to changing circumstances—and efficiency—by bypassing lengthy negotiations. Furthermore, auction technology is relatively easy to implement because it normally requires only one site installation: the seller can effectively impose the auction on the buyers, whereas other dynamic trading mechanisms, such as exchanges, require that both buyers and sellers first agree on the details of the protocol.

GENERAL PRINCIPLES OF AUCTION DESIGN

The auction designer's goal is to choose the right auction for the circumstances. In particular, the characteristics of the product (or service) that is being auctioned (whether it is private, common or correlated value) and of the bidder need to be taken into account when making this selection. Economic analysis provides an explanation of how this choice should take place. In particular, it can answer the question of what are the optimal bidding strategies given the design of the auction—that is, what is the Nash equilibrium?

Optimal bidding strategies provide an insight into the appropriate match between design and outcomes. A good example of this relationship is the very different experiences of the various European governments that sold third-generation mobile telephone licenses using auctions. Klemperer (2001) shows how the huge variation in the revenues raised by these auctions can be explained in terms of the quality of the match between the specific properties of the market—for example the number of licenses made available, the number of bidders—and the structure of the auction used.

Optimal bidding strategies in private value auctions

In a private value English auction, the actual bidding process conveys no relevant information to the bidders (other than determining who wins and how much they pay), because the value of the product for each bidder does not depend on how the others value it. Since there is no information in the actual bidding process, it is possible to determine in advance when to stop bidding. Stopping bidding below a bidder's reservation price is not rational because the item auctioned may still be won for a price lower than what it is worth to the bidder. Of course, it is not rational to bid above the reservation price, and so the bidder's optimal strategy is to stop bidding when the price is equal to her reservation price. This is true regardless of the bidding behavior of the other bidders, and so "stop bidding when the price equals your reservation price" is a dominant strategy.

In equilibrium, all bidders will use their dominant strategies. The winner will therefore be the bidder with the highest reservation price, and the price she pays will be equal to (slightly above, to be precise) the reservation price of the bidder with the second highest reservation value. Exactly how much above the second price the winning price is will depend on the rules of the auction, in particular on the minimal legal increment bidders are allowed to use, or—if the price is announced by an auctioneer—on the increments used by the auctioneer.

The English auction is strategically equivalent to a Vickrey auction. To see why, consider what a bidder with reservation price v should bid. Denote her bid by b. Whatever happens, the bidder will never be liable to pay her own bid. (She is liable to pay only if she wins the auction, but in a second-price sealed bid auction the winner pays the highest losing bid, not her own bid.) The bidder cannot gain by setting $b<v$, that is by bidding below her reservation price, because this will reduce her chances of winning the auction.

Vickrey's interesting observation was that the bidder also cannot gain from bidding $b>v$. To see why, recall that if the bidder wins the auction she has to pay the second highest bid. If this second highest bid is below v, then she cannot gain from bidding $b>v$ (because bidding v is sufficient to ensure winning in this case). But if this second-highest bid is above v, then she loses money by winning the auction, because she will have to pay a price for the item that is higher than what it is worth to her. She will actually be worst off bidding $b>v$ in this case. Hence the only rational bid would be $b=v$. Moreover, this is true independent of what bidding strategies are used by the other bidders. In game theory terms, bidding $b=v$ is a dominant strategy. Hence, the Vickrey auction is strategically equivalent to the English auction in the case of private values.

Once more, in equilibrium, all players will play their dominant strategies. The auction will therefore be won by the bidder with the highest reservation price, and the winner will pay the second highest reservation price. Hence the outcome of the Vickrey auction is also equivalent to that of an English auction.

The winner's curse and strategies for common value auctions

But this conclusion no longer holds if the item being auctioned is of common or correlated value. In this case, a bidder in an

English auction can actually learn about the value of the product by observing the bidding behavior of others. The bidder may want to revise her bidding strategy (that is, how much she is willing to pay) in light of what she observes in the auction. For example, if bidding is more aggressive than the bidder originally expected, she may decide to bid more. This type of behavior is of course not possible in a Vickrey auction (because bids are not observable). The English and Vickrey auctions therefore are not strategically equivalent if the value of the product or service auctioned is not private.

A general feature of common value auctions is the winner's curse. The winner is the person with the highest valuation for the item auctioned. But in a common value setting this is bad news, because the actual value of the item depends on how everyone else values it. Since everyone else clearly values it by less than the winner, this means that unless she shades her bid down in anticipation of this, she will end up paying more for the item than its real value. The winner's curse was first noted in the oil industry, where auctions are used to sell drilling rights in highly uncertain environments, and it has been verified in numerous experiments.

In a Dutch auction, the bidders decide in advance the price they will accept. The bidder who picked the highest price will win the auction (because she will be the first to bid), and will pay her bid. Hence the Dutch auction is strategically equivalent to the first-price sealed bid auction.

An important observation is that, in either of these auctions, it is *no longer* optimal to bid the true valuations. To see why, suppose that there are two bidders. Bidder A's reservation price for the item is $5. What should he bid in a first-price auction (sealed bid or Dutch)? How much to bid depends on his expectation of what his opponent will bid. If, for example, he expects that she will bid $2, then his optimal bid will be slightly above $2. Generally speaking, in first-price auctions bidders have incentives to shade their bids below the reservation price. The exact amount to bid can in fact be computed under more specific assumptions.[3]

---

[3] Bidding clearly depends on (1) the reservation prices of the other bidders, and (2) their bidding strategies. Finding the equilibrium of a first-price auction game-theoretically requires knowing the distribution according to which reservation prices are selected. This distribution needs to be common knowledge (that is, everyone has to know that reservation prices are selected according to this distribution, etc.). Finally, it is often necessary to restrict attention to the symmetric equilibrium, that is, to

Since agents do not have a dominant strategy in first-price auctions, bidding requires a certain amount of speculation (or reasoning about the likely behavior of others) and counter-speculation (taking account of how the other bidders are likely to reason about them). This makes the predictions of the theory less reliable, since it relies on a higher degree of reasoning by all participants.

The reason for this important difference between first-price and second-price auctions is as follows. A bid in a first-price auction needs to be chosen such that it:

- maximizes the chances of winning the auction,
- while at the same time minimizing how much the bidder pays in case she wins.

But these are clearly opposite forces—a higher bid increases the chances of winning, but commits the bidder to paying more if she wins. This conflict does not occur in a second-price auction because the bidder never pays her bid. (In a Vickrey auction the winner pays someone else's bid, and in an English auction the winner pays only slightly more than the second highest valuation.)

The general principle underlying second-price auctions can therefore be thought of as "separating what you say from what you pay".

Revenue equivalence

The most fundamental result in auction theory is the "revenue equivalence theorem". Roughly speaking, this theorem states that the expected revenues to the seller (or the buyer, in reverse auctions) is the same for a large number of auction forms, and that this conclusion holds under fairly unrestricted assumptions.[4] More specifically, all that is required from the auction design in order that the theorem applies is that:

- the design must ensure that the bidder with the high-

---

assume that all bidders use the same bidding strategies. See, e.g. Paul Klemperer's (1999) guide to the literature for more details, and for a numerical example in which the equilibrium strategies are computed.

4 In particular, the revenue equivalence theorem applies for private value auctions, and also for common value auctions, as long as the signals received by the bidders (that is, their information) are independent. Again, see Klemperer's (1999) survey for more details.

est valuation (or highest signal in a common value setting) wins the auction;

- the design must ensure that the bidder with the lowest valuation (signal) makes zero profits;
- the seller (or buyer in a reverse auction) and the bidders must be risk-neutral; that is that they must not be
  risk-averse or risk-loving.

Someone is risk-averse if he is willing to pay a premium to
avoid risk. Someone is risk-loving if he is willing to pay a premium for a bet. Suppose that you are offered a bet: you win $1
if a tossed coin comes out heads, and you pay $1 if it is tails. A
risk-neutral person is indifferent about participating in such an
auction. A risk-averse person will be willing to pay not to participate. A risk-lover will actually pay to play.

The four main auction types all satisfy the first two conditions and therefore are revenue equivalent. Furthermore, all
four auction types are also optimal—in the sense that they
maximize the revenue for the seller—as long as the seller uses
his optimal reserve price. [5]

Notice too that the revenues are the same, although the bidding behaviors are very different, in first and second-price
auctions. As is clear from the analysis of optimal bidding strategies, bids are typically higher in second-price auctions because
the optimal strategy is to bid the true valuation, whereas bids
are shaded down in first-price auctions. But in a second-price
auction the winner does not pay her own bid, but the second
highest. The revenue equivalence theorem states that in equilibrium (that is, when all bidders are rational) these effects
cancel out and the seller is, in expected terms, indifferent as to
which auction structure to use.

Attitudes to risk and the implications for auction design

The revenue equivalence theorem is a fundamental result in
auction theory, because it provides a method for comparing different auction formats. But the theorem does rely on the above
three assumptions, and while the first two are pretty harmless
(it is unlikely that any seller would want to use an auction that
does not satisfy these two conditions), the third condition is
often not met.

---

[5] The optimal reserve price depends, once more, on the distribution according to
which (independent) reservation values of bidders are drawn.

If, for example, the bidders are risk-averse, then the expected revenues from first-price auctions (Dutch or sealed bid) are higher than from second-price auctions (English or Vickrey). This is because risk aversion leads bidders to bid more aggressively in a first-price auction but does not affect bidding behavior in second-price auctions. [6] Along the same lines, if the seller is risk-averse (and the bidders are risk-neutral), then the expected revenue from using a second-price auction is higher than the expected revenue from using a first-price auction.

Consumers' fondness of the game-like feature of online auctions suggests that not only are they not risk-averse, but on the contrary they are risk-loving. In other words, they participate in the auction *because* it is a sort of a gamble. Focusing on Internet auctions, research by Dov Monderer and Moshe Tennenholtz (2000) suggests that sellers are in fact better off using third-price auctions (where the winner pays the third highest bid), because risk-loving bidders will bid even more aggressively in such auctions.

Although this suggestion has not yet been taken on board by online auctioneers, it may well indicate the shape of things to come. Certainly for relatively low price items, where bidders are likely to enjoy the thrill of bidding, the seller would be wise to use a second-price auction, such as an English auction. If and when third-price auctions become common, sellers would be wise to consider using them in these circumstances.

Finally, although the theory suggests that all main auction forms are revenue-equivalent, the designer will want to keep the auction as simple as possible. This is true for two reasons:

1. in order to attract bidders who will want to participate in the first place;
2. some features of the auction, such as the number of bidders and their exact attitude to risk, may not be known in advance.

It is therefore better to stick to a simple design that does not rely too much on these specific features. Since the English auc-

---

[6] Increasing the bid slightly in a first-price auction increases the probability of winning and decreases the payoff in case of winning. If bidding in a first-price sealed bid is thought of as participating in a lottery, then by bidding slightly more the bidder gets better odds with a slightly lower winning price. Since the bidder is risk-averse, she prefers security (less chance of losing or higher chance of winning) to higher prices. Hence she will bid more if she is risk-averse.

tion is known, both in theory and practice, to be robust (that is, to retain its revenue properties in a wide range of circumstances) and simple, it should be preferred, everything else being equal.

DESIGNING ONLINE AUCTIONS: THE PROBLEM OF LATE BIDDING

By far the most common auction protocol used on the web is the English, or ascending bid, auction. For example, David Lucking-Reiley's (2000) survey of 142 consumer auctions reveals that 121 (approximately 85 percent) were English auctions. Indeed, many people associate the term "auction" with an English auction. Paradoxically, the English auction is the only auction format of the four main auction types that cannot be implemented on the web in its original form. This is because an online auction must have a closing date: otherwise new bidders, and new bids, can, in theory, continue to arrive forever. It turns out that this feature has a considerable impact on bidding behavior.

Bidders in Internet auctions bid by remote control. Sellers therefore need to announce a closing time, a deadline by which the auction ends. Such a deadline is not necessary in an offline English auction, because all the bidders are physically present and so the auction can run its course (that is, until there is only one bidder left) within a relatively short period of time. For example, Sotheby's auctions take a few minutes, and rarely more than an hour, while most agriculture auctions for livestock and fresh produce take only a few seconds for each item.

If an English auction is run in its original form, with a deadline, then bidders have an incentive to bid late. If the price is still low close to the deadline, then it may be possible to win the auction in the last minute with a relatively low bid. Moreover, if most bidders bid late, the price will rise more slowly, which in turn will increase the incentives to bid late.

In comparison, forcing a closing date on a Dutch auction or on any sealed bid auction (first or second-price) does not affect bidding. In the former, the first to bid wins anyway, and so behavior does not matter. And the latter comes with a deadline anyhow—the closing dates for bids.

The problem of late bidding is unique to English auctions and can result in lower revenues for the sellers. In addition, many bids arriving in the closing minutes or seconds of the auction can cause congestion and delay when implemented on the web. Once again, this can result in lower revenues, because a high bid may be delayed and miss the deadline, so that the auction will close at a lower price.

There are two methods that are currently being used to avoid the late bidding problem:

- proxy bidding;
- automatic extension of the auction's closing time.

With the proxy bidding solution, people do not bid for objects directly. Instead, they submit a reservation (maximum) price, which is used as a basis of bidding on their behalf. The bid submitted to the auction registers not as the person's reservation price, but rather as an incremental amount above the highest bid at the time. As further bids are made, the person's bid rises incrementally until it is the highest bid left or it reaches the bidder's reservation price. If all bidders submit their true reservation prices, the English auction becomes a Vickrey auction; the theoretical properties of the auction are then maintained and the problem of late bidding is resolved.

The second solution is automatically to extend the auction closing time if a bid is received in the last stages of the auction. This approach is used in the vast majority of B2B auctions and also in some consumer auctions, such as those run by Amazon.

At the core of this book is an emphasis on the relationship between the details of trading mechanisms and the behavior of self-interested agents. It is interesting therefore to look at the relationship between an auction's structure and the resulting bidding behavior. To do this, it is useful to compare the bidding in two auctions with the same structure apart from the strictness in deadlines to see whether any differences arise.

Amazon and eBay, which both carry out Internet auctions, offer this opportunity since they have the same structure except that eBay has strict deadlines while Amazon's are more flexible. Both eBay and Amazon use second-price auctions, where economic theory suggests that the dominant strategy for bidders is to bid their true reservation price. But what is found in many Internet auctions is that many bids are placed in the auction's closing seconds, which suggests that bidders are not submitting their true reservation price earlier in the auction. Such behavior seems odd, since the advice from both auctioneers and sellers is that bidders should simply submit their maximum willingness to pay for the object being auctioned. For example, eBay advises its bidders to submit their true reservation price early in the auction:

eBay always recommends bidding the absolute maximum that one is willing to pay for an item early in the auction. ... if one is outbid, one should be, at worst, ambivalent toward being outbid. After all, someone else was simply willing to pay more than you wanted to pay for it.

Sellers also urge potential buyers to place their bids early, as late bids run the risk of not being transmitted successfully. The following is representative of advice given by sellers:

The danger of last minute bidding: almost without fail after an auction has closed we receive e-mails from bidders who claim they were attempting to place a bid and were unable to get into eBay. ... All we can do in this regard is to urge you to place your bids early. If you're serious in your intent to become a winning bidder please avoid eBay's high traffic during the close of an auction.

In trying to assess why bidding behavior might exhibit such tendencies, a natural experiment presents itself. Both eBay and Amazon carry out auctions over the Internet but have different rules. In auctions at Amazon, if a bid is made in the last 10 minutes the auction is automatically extended so that it does not end until 10 minutes after the last bid is made. The deadlines are thus quite flexible. Auctions at eBay, on the other hand, have rigid deadlines.

Incentives to bid late

Research by Roth and Ockenfels (2000b) indicates that there is considerably more late bidding on eBay than on Amazon. It also shows that more experienced bidders on eBay are more likely to bid late, while on Amazon the opposite is true.

There is a positive probability that last minute bids will fail to register in an Internet auction. Thus, there is an incentive to bid early. But there is also an incentive not to bid too high when there is time left for other bidders to place higher bids, that is, to avoid a bidding war that will raise the expected final price. Roth and Ockenfels's analysis suggests a number of possible explanations for late bidding in Internet auctions. These can be divided into two broad categories.

- First, there is what they call "non-strategic" late bidding. Bidders delay their bidding for no special reason, or because they prefer not to leave bids hanging, or because search engines present soon-to-expire auctions first. The predicted contribution to late bidding of such non-strategic bidders is that there should be no difference in late bidding between Amazon and eBay.

- Second, bidders bid late for strategic reasons; that is, they are responding optimally to their beliefs about the behavior of other bidders.

Roth and Ockenfels suggest three possible causes of strategic late bidding:

1. avoiding bidding wars: bidders bid late to avoid bidding wars with other like-minded bidders;
2. avoiding naïve bidding: bidders bid late as a rational response to naive English auction behavior, i.e. to avoid bidding wars with naive bidders;
3. late bidding by experts: informed bidders attempt to protect their information.

Avoiding bidding wars
Consider an auction with two bidders, each of which has quite a high reservation price for the product. If one bids early in the auction, the other could respond by bidding slightly higher. If this process continued, the price eventually paid for the product would rise. This might discourage either of them from bidding early so as to avoid pushing the price up. This effect would be more pronounced in auctions with strict deadlines, since if the deadline is flexible bidding early or late makes less difference as there is always time for the other bidder to respond.

The predicted contribution this would have to late bidding is therefore that there would be more late bidding on eBay than on Amazon. There should also be a bigger effect for more experienced bidders.

Avoiding naïve bidders
Some users confuse eBay's second-price auction with a standard English auction, where bidding is direct, and where bidders are required to raise their bids in response to price changes. If such bidders are present, then it is better to bid late to avoid bidding wars with them.

The predicted contribution to late bidding here is that there would be more late bidding in categories of goods in which expertise in bidding is important, for example antiques.

Late bidding by experts

Consider an auction for an item with ambiguous value. Assume there are two bidders, one who is an expert and one who is not. The uninformed bidder will be unsure of the value of the item and so will look to the actions of the expert as a signal of quality. If the expert bids early, it is quite possible that the uninformed bidder could take that as a signal of good quality and go on to outbid the expert. The expert therefore has an incentive to keep his information to himself until near the end of the auction, when there is less chance of uninformed bidders being able to outbid him. Obviously, such behavior is more likely to occur in auctions for goods that do not have an obvious retail value, as only then is there a real premium on being an expert.

Here again, the prediction is that there would be more late bidding in categories of goods where expertise is important.

Evidence on the timing of late bids

To assess these hypotheses, Roth and Ockenfels (2000a) looked at the timing of bids on Amazon and eBay, and also compared different categories of auctions, like antiques and computers, which have different scope for expert information.

In both auction houses, a significant proportion of last bids are submitted in the final hour of the auction. But late bidding happens far more frequently on eBay than on Amazon. Furthermore, within that final hour, eBay bids are far more concentrated in the last few minutes than Amazon bids, regardless of the category of the auction item. This suggests that bidders are refraining from placing bids earlier in the auction in order to avoid a bidding war. When questioned about why they bid late, most bidders confirm that late bidding is a part of their planned strategy, explaining it in terms of trying to avoid a bidding war or generally trying to keep the price down.

This pattern of late bidding is exaggerated when looking at experienced bidders are studied. With experienced bidders, an even higher proportion of bids is put in late to eBay, while the opposite is true for Amazon. This would suggest that last minute bidding behavior is not simply due to naïve behavior, but to bidders' responding strategically to the structure of the auction.

Furthermore, significantly more late bidding is seen in antiques auctions than in computer auctions. This suggests that bidding behavior also responds to the strategic incentives created by the possession of information about the item being sold. When questioned, experienced antiques bidders often state that late bidding enables them to avoid sharing their valuable information with the other bidders. As one experienced antiques bidder explained:

> The most difficult part is ascertaining the genuineness of a particular piece. ... This is where it is important not to bid early on an item. If you are well known as an expert and you bid, then you have authenticated the item for free and invite bidding by others.

But there is also some evidence of naïve late bidding on eBay and Amazon. A few bidders, generally inexperienced, seem to confuse eBay with an English auction. Instead of letting a software program do the bidding, they start low and submit a new bid every time someone else outbids them. Also, some bidders seem to feel the need to be listed as the high bidder and so keep bidding until their money runs out. An experienced bidder said of inexperienced bidders:

> If there is a first time bidder then it's best to walk away. They will push the price up just to stay the high bidder.

It seems as though late bidding is usually a part of a planned strategy. But the reasons for late bidding vary across bidders. Some explain it as being because they want to avoid a bidding war, some because they have information they do not want to signal to other bidders, and some because they are simply inexperienced.

To summarize, late bidding on Internet auctions can have multiple causes. The difference in the amount of late bidding on eBay and Amazon indicates that strategic considerations play a significant role. Since eBay's auctions have a strict closing time, there is more reason for bidders to bid late in order to keep the price down. This observation is strengthened by its exaggeration when looking at more experienced bidders.

The difference in the extent of late bidding for computers and antiques implies that bidders respond to the additional strategic incentives for late bidding in markets where expertise is important in valuing the item. But the significant amount of late bidding on Amazon suggests there are also non-strategic causes of late bidding. This can be explained at least partly by there being naïve or inexperienced bidders.

The research suggests that automatically extending the deadline if bids arrive in the final 5 minutes eliminates much of the problem of late bidding.

ADDITIONAL ISSUES FOR ONLINE AUCTION DESIGNERS

The problem of late bidding in second-price auctions is a good example of the new set of problems encountered by bidders and designers alike when implementing and participating in auctions in an e-commerce setting. Since English auctions constitute the vast majority of online auctions, the problem has received a great deal of attention and is now relatively well understood.

But there are a number of other issues relating to online auctions, particularly in the context of business auctions, where existing theory does not provide sufficient insight into bidding behavior. Since auction design is based on an understanding of how bidders behave (or, more precisely, on the assumption that bidders will use their equilibrium bidding strategies), the impact of these issues on profits and design is still largely unknown.

Delays

In the original Dutch auction for flowers, bidders are physically located in the same room and press a button to place a bid. But when such an auction is implemented on the web, it is possible that there will be a delay between the "button pressing" of a bidder and the time when the bid is received by the auctioneer (or seller). When Dutch auctions started appearing on the web, this emerged as a problem. For example, it is possible that when the price was 5, a bidder pressed the button, but his bid was delayed and then another bidder won the auction with a lower bid, say 4, because her bid was not delayed.

Dutch auctions are used to sell crates of fish in the Barcelona fish market. A team of computer scientists in Barcelona implemented this auction on the web (see Rodríguez et al., 1997). Buyers placed bids through a communication device or a computer screen. Once the problem of delayed bids was acknowledged, a number of solutions were tested to solve it. One effective solution is to use a synchronization protocol (interestingly, many of these protocols were developed to allow multi-player web-based computer games) to control the flow of bids and announcements. This completely eliminated the problem, but comes at the price of slowing the auction. The solution chosen will typically depend on the exact requirements of the e-commerce application for which the Dutch auction is going to be used.

Finding out the value of the item

Economic analysis assumes that buyers know the value of the item themselves and bid accordingly. But this assumption does not always hold, even if the product sold is of private value. The reason is that the complexity of computing this value may be so high that the bidder is unlikely to carry out such calculations. This is particularly true in multi-item auctions, where bidders bid for various combinations of goods and services.

For example, bidders in the U.S. auction of mobile communication licenses could place bids for any combination of states. But the worth of acquiring these licenses depended on many parameters (for example the number of people living in each state, and the density of the population in areas covered by the licenses), including the proximity of states. So the value of each "bundle" of states needed to be computed separately. But if bidders do not know the exact value of each possible combination of items, it is difficult for them to calculate how much they should bid and more generally to predict the outcome of the auction. Without a good understanding of how people bid, it is difficult to design efficient auctions in such cases. Further research on this is needed before effective auctions can be designed.

Complexity in large business auctions

Large business auctions are most likely in the context of e-procurement, for example the purchasing of raw materials and of indirect materials such as office supplies. Since most companies use e-procurement systems, the efforts of purchasers can shift away from manual requisition and payment processing. This opportunity is illustrated by a study of over 1,000 billion-dollar companies by the Hackett Group, which shows that approximately 76 percent of the procurement professional's efforts is devoted to requisition, order, receipt and payment processing, and only an estimated 2 percent of effort is devoted to strategic negotiations with trading partners. The wide use of auctions is likely to change this ratio. Purchasers can now devote the majority of their time to strategic issues, such as who to buy from and what price to pay.

The importance of improving the effectiveness of purchasers in such strategic tasks is obvious. A dollar saved is an extra dollar in the bottom line (as opposed to an increase in sales, for example, where an additional dollar is typically worth far less in the bottom line). A typical billion-dollar company spends at least 40 percent of revenues on purchased goods and services. Therefore, any improvement in procurement's spending effectiveness translates into significant shareholder value.

However, business auctions also *complicate* the decisions of purchasers considerably. First, auctions privilege those players with strong bargaining power, which in many cases are sellers (i.e. the purchaser is *forced* to buy through seller-run auctions). It is technically simpler for a seller to force an auction on suppliers than it is for a buyer to run a reverse auction. The reason for this is the difficulty of automatically modeling preferences over the various attributes of the product or service auctioned. Since most business transactions involve more than just price, this problem turns out to be significant. The asymmetry in running auctions is the main reason why buyers are sometimes worse off using e-commerce.

Further sources of complexity are now discussed in more detail.

Limited capacity in business auctions
Online auctions are often used to sell surplus stocks. In such cases, the quantity auctioned is typically fixed and limited (e.g. "you must bid for all 70 units"). In these settings, buyers will need to allocate purchases between several sellers. Bidding in each of these auctions should therefore be part of a global bidding strategy. How much to bid in one auction will depend on prices and quantities available from other sellers. Bidding behavior in such environments is not explained by existing economic theory.

Bidding in simultaneous auctions
Along the same lines, buyers may find themselves bidding in a number of auctions, possibly simultaneously. This may happen because the quantity sold in any one auction is not enough, or because the same item is being sold at a number of auctions and the buyer is trying to win the auction with the lowest price. Clearly, the maximum bid in one auction will depend on the chances of winning the other auction(s) using, for example, a lower price. Bidding elves, currently offered to buyers in many auction sites, cannot handle this complexity. Once again, what constitutes optimal bidding in one auction will depend on what happens in the other auctions.

Bidding and negotiating
A global purchasing strategy can involve bidding in an auction and at the same time negotiating with one or more vendors for the same items. In this setting, how much to bid in the auction will depend once more on the current state of negotiations.

Taking advantage of scale economics
Suppose that the organization requires an unusually large quantity of a certain product or service. Should it make this known to potential sellers or not? Sometimes making this information public can be beneficial because the buyer can demand a discount for bulk buying. In the extreme, the buyer can create a reverse auction where potential sellers submit bids. On the other hand, there will be other cases where the buyer is better off not revealing the fact that the firm requires a large quantity. Substantial increases in demand may drive prices up, and the organization may end up paying more than it would have paid, had the information be kept secret.

Computing the value of deal
The buyer will need to evaluate what the deal is actually worth for the organization (for example, the maximum price it is willing to pay for 20 tons of cement). Naturally, this worth may change depending on many factors: how badly the company needs these items, the availability and price of close substitutes, and fall-back contracts the organization may have with its competitors. Bidding and buying strategies will depend on this value, and should be flexible enough to adapt to any relevant changes in the expected worth of future deals.

Action–reaction
The outcome of a decision to buy from A rather than B will depend on how A and B react. For example, it would not be wise to lose the "valued customer" status with A for a small, one-off discount from B. Similarly, how much to bid in an auction will normally depend on how much the other buyers are likely to bid. These types of speculation can considerably increase the complexity of making buying decisions.

Multi-attributes
Most business-to-business transactions depend not only on price, but also on other attributes, such as quantities available, quality assurances, guaranteed time to delivery and after-sale

support. Each option of where and how much to buy will need to be evaluated using a multi-dimensional scale, which weighs the various relevant attributes according to the organization's preferences. Once more, this increases the complexity of the decision rule.

Solutions

All of these issues contribute to the complexity of participating in business auctions. Buyers will need to adapt to the fact that the same goods will be sold at different prices on different days (because what determines prices is the winning bid, and this is likely to change). Decision support software tools can help address the problem of complexity. Such tools, especially if they are designed for corporate purchasers, can reduce this complexity and improve the bidding precision of corporate purchasers.

There have already been some attempts in this direction. Companies such as Perfect.com and Commerce One are developing software for precision bidding. The e-Services Markets Department at the Hewlett–Packard (HP) laboratories is carrying out the most comprehensive research in this area. The team is focusing on the need to automate the negotiation process between trading partners in business e-commerce. It has already developed many technologies for automated negotiations, protocols and marketplaces. In particular, the team holds a number of patents for algorithms for simultaneous bidding in auctions and negotiations.

One of the technologies developed by HP is a real-time optimization tool called "Negotia: The Assistant Corporate Purchaser".[7] Negotia is designed to empower corporate buyers in response to changes in the purchasing process resulting from e-procurement and supply chain automation, such as the ones described above. Negotia is a decision support tool: it acts as an online economic consultant for the organization, recommending buying strategies. Specifically, given a certain request from the user, and on the basis of current market conditions and relevant history, Negotia is designed to address the following questions: Who to buy from? How much to buy from each of these sellers? Should the organization try to negotiate a better deal and, if so, how? The system supports multi-vendor interactions, bidding in simultaneous auctions and multiple direct

---

[7] Nir Vulkan developed the original concept for Negotia. HP owns the current version.

negotiations. It provides the user (the purchaser) with real-time optimizations of purchasing decisions (figure 7.1).

Negotia is based on game-theoretical and dynamic programming techniques. Much of its ability to provide the purchaser with accurate information stems from its model of the preferences of the purchasing organization. While there have been attempts to model the purchasing organization's preferences (notably by ExperCommerce.com and Perfect.com), these focused on dynamically constructing preferences. In contrast, Negotia does the preference modeling offline, during a customization phase. It then allows online negotiation support in

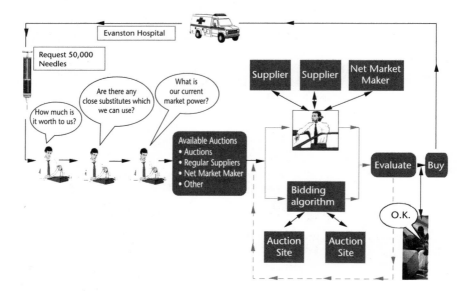

Figure 7.1: Example of a Negotia purchase

First, an order is generated, for example via an ERP or an e-procurement system. Next, Negotia estimates the worth of the deal for the organization, checks substitutes and evaluates its current negotiation position. Negotia generates a search pattern for auctions where the requested product or service can be purchased. It then makes its "first stab" at computing optimal trading strategy, proceeds to generate requests to vendors and then re-evaluates the action space according to first results of negotiations. Negotiation and bidding continue until a satisfactory outcome is reached. Finally, Negotia recommends who to buy from and for how much.

a price-dynamic environment. As a result, Negotia is much more suitable for the purchasing of raw materials and commodities, where the organization's preferences are largely fixed, and where online negotiations and bidding is the key issue in strategic purchasing.

More specifically, Negotia maintains a representation of the *permanent* preferences of an organization in different situations. Information is kept on product preferences e.g. price, quantity, brand, technical specification, terms of delivery. Furthermore, the system maintains the necessary *market* information for making purchasing decisions. It stores information about demand, sellers, additional buyers who may affect demand, supply schedules, historical data, existence of close substitutes, exchange mechanisms, etc.

Negotia is an example of a new generation of e-commerce applications designed in response to changes in the way organizations interact. They are based on economic or game-theoretical techniques. As the use of automated negotiations and auctions increases, the demand for such tools is likely to increase. In the future it is likely that these tools will become standard commerce tools, in much the same way as spreadsheets and word processors are used today.

KEY CONSIDERATIONS FOR ONLINE AUCTIONS
What designers need to think about

- Prefer dominant-strategy designs: prefer second-price auctions to first-price auctions (separate what bidders say from what they pay), everything else being equal.
- Prefer simple designs, so that bidders can easily figure out what their optimal bidding strategy is and will therefore be more likely to attain equilibrium. Prefer English auctions, everything else being equal.
- Take into account the type of object (or service) that is being auctioned—distinguish between private, common and correlated value objects.
- Carry out an equilibrium analysis and use the equilibrium as the prediction of the likely outcome.
- In a second-price auction, an extended deadline is better than a fixed deadline in dealing with late bidders.
- Consider carefully whether the design suggested can be implemented on the Web as it is (for example, make sure delays are not a problem).

What market participants need to know

- Bidding in first-price auctions depends on your belief about what the others are likely to bid. Always bid below your valuation.
- Bidding your true valuation is a dominant strategy in a second-price auction (English or Vickrey).
- Avoid the winner's curse: in common value auctions, take into account the fact that you will win only if you have the highest estimate of the real value—bid below your estimate.
- If there is a strict deadline, consider bidding late, to take advantage of possible lower closing prices. But if the auction has an automatic extension, bid your true valuation.
- Bidding for multi-units: consider all your options. How much to bid in one auction should depend on the price(s) you expect to get in the other auctions or in direct negotiations with sellers.

Chapter 8

Many-to-many Electronic Exchanges

INTRODUCTION

An *exchange* is an economic mechanism bringing together buyers and sellers. This definition includes anything from bulletin boards to stock exchanges. The key difference between electronic exchanges and the mechanisms discussed in the previous chapters is that in the former there are potentially many buyers and many sellers. While auctions and direct negotiations currently account for the majority of business-to-business transactions, for most goods and services there are, at any given point in time, many potential buyers and sellers who could trade via an exchange—if one existed. This chapter address the design issues involved in setting up many-to-many e-commerce exchanges.

Encouraged by the prospects of creating "Nasdaq-type" exchanges for almost all types of product, herds of entrepreneurs and investors launched a large number of web-based exchanges in the second half of the 1990s supported by huge market valuations. In 1999 alone it is estimated that more than 700 B2B marketplaces were launched for anything from steel to chemicals. The aspiration of having, for every product and service, a stock-exchange type market where prices are set according to the current state of demand and supply, seemed to be within reach.

By early 2001, however, it became clear that this vision might have been too optimistic. *The Economist*, for example, reported a study by the consultancy AMR Research, which found that not a single one of the 600 B2B exchanges studied had reached even 1 percent of the overall trading volume in its industry. Why had these businesses not taken off as expected? This chapter attempts to address this question.

First, however, we need to understand how exchanges operate, how they are created, and the incentives of participants to join them. We also need to provide the designers of e-commerce exchanges with the basic theoretical tools to create and maintain such markets. Toward the end of the chapter we discuss the possibility of automating trading, by providing traders with software agents. The chapter describes Hewlett–Packard's "Jester" experiments on human–agent interface in exchange trading, and draws conclusions for the future use of such a technology. It ends with a case study of electronic communications networks (ECNs) and the effect they had on security trading in the United States in the second half of the 1990s.

WHAT CAN BE TRADED THROUGH AN EXCHANGE?

There are now Web-based exchanges for a huge range of goods and services. A recent survey by Lasester, Long and Capers (2001) found 1,802 e-marketplaces in industries as varied as agriculture, paper, printing, energy, transportation/logistics, food, electronics, retail, automotive, telecom, chemicals and aerospace, to name but a few.

While some of these e-marketplaces extend traditional markets, others, such as the market for bandwidth, consist of a totally new type of transaction. The background to this particular market is the deregulation of the telecommunications industry and the explosive growth of the Internet (with its "bandwidth-thirsty" applications), which changed the supply and demand landscape for telecoms capacity. These changes have also increased the number of players at both ends of the supply and demand spectrum.

Traffic requirements for Internet service providers have been doubling every 72 days in recent months. The traditional bilateral nature of buyer–seller relationships is inefficient as well as impractical. In the past, Internet service providers were forced to buy capacity for an entire year and ran the risk of getting stuck with excess capacity while waiting for the demand to catch up with their supply. Meanwhile, market rates on bandwidth have been falling at around 32 percent per year.

As a consequence, bandwidth exchanges have emerged to provide a marketplace for the multilateral trading of bandwidth capacity. In addition to the actual physical transaction of bandwidth, a neutral exchange market can also provide financial instruments (derivatives such as forwards and options) for a telecommunications business to hedge against price fluctuations and availability uncertainties.

RateXchange is a good example of an online marketplace for buying, selling and delivering wholesale bandwidth. It is a B2B e-commerce company that provides a neutral, vertical marketplace for the telecommunications industry. It provides a complete service to its members, including an electronic exchange that facilitates the entire transaction between participating carriers. This electronic marketplace constitutes a central point of contact and interconnection that matches buyers' and sellers' orders and fulfils transactions using a standardized contract that includes quality of service and payment terms.

Standardization

In order for an exchange to work, the product or service that is being traded must be standardized (or commoditized). Negotiations over anything other than price (or price per fixed quantity) must become unnecessary. If the underlying contract is complex, possibly involving a technical specification, then firms will insist on negotiating the various attributes directly with each other. Moreover, there is likely to be industry pressure toward long-term relationships where quality of service and technical compatibility are guaranteed. (So an exchange for a highly specified piece of equipment is unlikely to work.)

One of the reasons exchanges for bandwidth are successful is that bandwidth, like wheat and gold, is a relatively homogeneous product: once the quantity is fixed, price is the only variable that the trading parties need to agree upon.

Most of the "dot com boom" electronic exchanges failed because the underlying transactions were not easy to standardize. According to *The Economist*, an estimated 80–90 percent of all business goods and services are actually traded through extended-term contracts, often lasting for a year or more. The public "spot" markets, which quote up-to-the-minute prices, are just the tiny tip of a huge private market of one-to-one contract deals, which are hard to bring onto the Internet.

An understanding of how the industry works is crucial before any attempt to standardize contracts can take place. Too many electronic exchanges have failed for this lesson to be ignored. For instance, *The Economist* reports on the start-up company GoCargo (founded 1998), which manages an exchange for the container shipping industry. Containers are commodity-like:

they come in standard-sized, sealed units. As *The Economist* put it, "If ever there was a product perfect for online trading, this seemed to be the one." However, the company was not an immediate success. It turns out that shippers really want an end-to-end solution: someone who would take care not only of the sea part of the container's journey, but also its land journey, by truck or train, and customs on both ends of the journey. Shippers are willing to pay more to a logistics firm than to buy cheaply on the exchange and have to take care of the remaining aspects of the journey themselves. Furthermore, although the container itself is standard, buyers and sellers worry about reliability and long-term relationships, which insure availability over a set period. Another problem is that deals in the container industry tend to be "conditional". A carrier will agree to move containers in one direction only if it can find someone who will pay it to bring them back again. Unless online exchanges can accommodate these types of problem, they will be ignored.

Notwithstanding these problems, one can find commodities in one form or another in the production chain of almost any product. For example, PC manufacturers use standard memory sticks and motherboards. Food companies buy wheat and cocoa beans. Soft drinks producers buy sugar and aluminium for cans, publishers buy paper, and so on.

However, even if the underlying product is standard, there still remains the issue of whether it is purchased on its own, or as part of a package (e.g. container space as part of a door-to-door logistic service). If it is purchased as part of a package, then the exchange must either provide the same services (but then the total package may no longer be standard!) or not. If it does not, it must deliver substantial savings to purchasers in order to persuade them to change the way they work. Detailed industry knowledge is required to be able to make these decisions. Exchanges that do not rely on the advice of industry experts are more likely to fail.

Similar issues arise if the underlying product varies in quality, or if the level of service matters. (For example, is a ton of aluminium the same whoever sells it, or do purchasers pay extra to buy from a reputable seller?) It will be bad business for the exchange to be branded as the place to get cheap but low-quality goods. The problem of adverse selection, described in chapter 5, can prove devastating in such circumstances.

Finally, after overcoming all the above issues, the exchange must establish its actual trading rules.

HOW DO EXCHANGES WORK?

Exchanges bring together buyers and sellers to facilitate trade. There are two broad types of exchange: those that set a clearing-price, and those that do not. A *call market* is a good general example of an exchange that does set a clearing price. Although the exact rules may differ slightly between exchanges, the general principles are always the same. In a call market traders submit bids and offers. The market then collects these bids and offers and constructs supply and demand curves. Based on these curves, the market computes a market-clearing price, and executes the indicated trades.

For example, suppose that there are six buyers and seven sellers. The buyers submit the following bids: $2, $3, $6, $7, $8 and $10. The sellers submit the following offers: $2, $4, $5, $8, $9, $11 and $13. Figure 8.1, which lists price on the vertical axis and quantity on the horizontal axis, shows the demand and supply curve corresponding to these numbers.

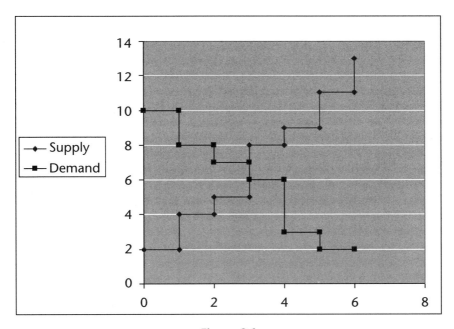

Figure 8.1

The diagram can be read as follows. If the price is below $2, no one is willing to sell the product. At any price between $2 and $4, there will be exactly one seller who is willing to sell. At a price between $4 and $5, there will be two sellers willing to sell; and so on. Similarly, the demand curve is interpreted as follows. If the price is higher than $10, then no one is willing to buy. At a price between $10 and $8, there is one buyer (the buyer with the willingness to pay $10); and so on.

The demand and supply curves intercept when the price is between $6 and $7. Any price between these two can serve as a market-clearing price. For example, the call market can split the difference (this mechanism is known as a "$\frac{1}{2}$ double auction"), and set the market-clearing price at $6.5. Now the three buyers with the highest bids ($10, $8 and $7) trade with the three sellers with the lowest offers ($2, $4 and $5) at a price of $6.5. The others do not trade.

The daily opening price of each stock listed on the New York Stock Exchange is set by a call market that aggregates the bids and offers that have arrived overnight. In London call markets are used twice a day to fix copper and gold prices. The Wunsch system of computerized trading conducts periodic call markets in each of the listed stocks of the New York Stock Exchange. Prior to the auction cut-off time (i.e. the time by which bids must arrive), traders are sometimes allowed to cancel or replace orders entered, but are typically penalized for doing so. For example, the Arizona Stock Exchange charges two commissions (both buy and sell side) for replacing a bid with a less aggressive one (lower bid or higher offer). After the market clears, traders are normally allowed to revise their bid before the next cut-off time where the new market-clearing price is computed.

Other exchanges do not set a clearing price. Instead they simply act as an intermediary, facilitating trade between buyers and sellers, who negotiate the final details of the trade (e.g. the price) off-line. It is also possible for an exchange to offer both services to traders. This is somewhat similar to what happens in some European stock exchanges, like London and Paris, where traders can trade via "the floor", where some sort of a market-clearing mechanism is typically used, or on "the second floor", where trade takes place through one-to-one negotiations.

In the long run, e-exchanges that set prices are most likely to survive. Already sites using price setting rules, like the U.S. Treasury market and Cantor Fitzergerald's e-speed site (for trading bonds), seem to be doing much better than their competitors. This is no coincidence: the following section explains the economic benefits from setting prices.

Should the exchange set prices?

Exchanges that set clearing prices have a number of important advantages over exchanges where traders are left to negotiate directly. First, it removes from traders the burden of multiple one-to-one negotiations. Since negotiations can be costly in terms of time and effort, this is an important advantage. Second, and this is a point already made in chapter 4, one-to-one negotiations are informationally inefficient; that is, rational buyers and sellers may end up not trading in cases where economic efficiency requires that they do. More specifically, because it is rational for a buyer to pretend she is willing to pay less than she really is, and similarly for a seller to pretend to want a higher price than his real valuation, then they often do not trade even though it is mutually beneficial. Chapter 4 also explained why exchanges that set prices significantly reduce the incentives of traders to act strategically, i.e. to manipulate their bids and asks. Using the call auction example from above, we can now return to this point in more detail.

Can any of the traders in this example gain by manipulating their bids? Only the buyer who bid $7 and the seller who bid $5 affect the clearing price. The buyer who bid $7 *can* gain by bidding less—for instance if she bids $6.5 then the clearing price will be $6.25—a gain of $0.25. However, if she bids less than $6 her bid will no longer be the marginal bid, and she will not trade. Similarly, the seller who bid $5 can gain by bidding more, because this will increase the clearing price (but if he bids more than $8 they will not trade). So exactly one buyer and one seller can gain by not bidding their true valuations.

For all other buyers and sellers, telling the truth is the best strategy, since it ensures that a seller will trade only if the clearing price is above his (real) acceptable threshold, or that a buyer will trade only if it is below her real willingness to pay. For example, suppose that the real valuation of the seller who bid $9 is $4. By pretending that he is "tougher" than he really is, the seller takes the risk that he will not trade, because his bid is too high. Conditional of the clearing price being set independently of its own bid, the seller is best off bidding his true valuation.

Of course, traders do not know in advance what the other bids are, and therefore must decide their bids and asks before they know what the others are doing. The exact decision rule is complex—it depends among other things on the trader's beliefs about the actual reservation prices of the others and on the strategies they are using. Nevertheless, it is relatively easy to see that if a trader believes her bid is unlikely to be marginal, then she has little incentive to manipulate it. Moreover, whether a trader's bid is marginal is related to the total number of traders. As the number of traders' increase, the *ex ante* probability that a given trader will be marginal becomes very small, and so the incentives to "lie" become negligible.

In a seminal paper from 1994, Rustichini, Satterthwaite and Williams (RSW), formally analyze the one-shot call auction game, and compute the equilibrium bid–ask structure. They find that the call auction game exhibits a continuum of equilibria, but that in *all* these equilibria the difference between each and every trader's real valuation and their equilibrium bid or ask decreases as the number of traders increases. Furthermore, RSW show that the rate at which this difference decreases is fast: even in markets with as few as three or four buyers and sellers, the difference between real valuations and equilibrium bids and asks is negligibly small. RSW further compared the rate at which these differences become small between various many-to-many trading mechanisms. They found that the call auction market converges to truth-telling faster than all other trading mechanisms.

The RSW result can be interpreted as follows. Exchanges that use a call auction are the most information efficient [1] devices to trade between privately informed traders. In other words, call auctions—more than any other trading mechanisms—provide traders with the correct incentives to bid truthfully.

Price-setting exchanges, like call auctions, can also lead to an efficient allocation of resources in an economy. The basic premise is this. A seller posts a price; if he sees excess demand, he raises the price; if he sees excess supply, he lowers the price. The price, therefore, reflects the terms of trade between goods, and indicates to manufacturers whether they should increase or reduce production.

Furthermore, participants often have diverse information about the future; for example, if the underlying product traded is a commodity, such as oil or metal, manufacturers may have private information about their future production capacities.

---

[1] Where information efficiency is defined as the ability to overcome problems associated with private information. In other words, a trading mechanism is information efficient if it facilitates trade between a buyer and a seller every time the buyer's (maximal) willingness to pay is higher than the seller's (minimal) accepted price.

Similarly, buyers know more about future demand; and so on. In a price-setting exchange where clearing prices can be observed by traders, they can learn each other's information by observing prices, and change their actions according to the prices they see. By doing so, the diverse information available is aggregated into a single price. If the price does not reflect a given trader's beliefs about the value of the product, the trader will conclude that others know something he does not, and update his views.

These positive effects are not present when the exchange does not set prices, because traders do not observe the aggregated demand and supply information. Instead they know only the outcomes of transactions where they themselves were involved. A key issue, therefore, is whether the exchange does indeed aggregate all available information, and the speed with which it does so. An exchange is said to be *informationally efficient* when the prices *fully and instantaneously* reflect all available relevant information. This is the case in most financial markets, where trade takes place often and where traders can view clearing prices in real-time. In designing an exchange, efficiency can be encouraged through an appropriate choice of information dissemination policy.

What information should the exchange disseminate?

There are various types of data an exchange can choose to release, for example the price, quantity, time and identities of the parties of last trade; the high, low, opening and closing trading prices; the best bid–ask prices and their quantities, parties; etc. Which of these data will be disseminated will depend on the specific needs and ownership structure of the exchange. There are however two general recommendations that can be drawn.

First, disseminating the identities of traders will almost always be bad for the exchange. It is normally not in the best interest of the trader that its business becomes public. (If you are selling cheap because you need to, you might prefer to remain anonymous.) Clearly, the exchange needs to protect its members' interests. The exchange will also wish to avoid the phenomenon of parties meeting on the system but trading off it, thereby avoiding the exchange's fees and/or commission.

This last point is true in general. There is always a conflict between disseminating information in order to attract trading on the one hand, and making off-exchange trading, with its consequent avoidance of charges and exchange rules, easier on the other. Off-exchange trading also reduces the possible value of the data which the exchange might want to consider selling as an additional source of income. For example, if yours is a membership-based exchange you could make money by selling trading data to companies in the industry who are not members of the exchange. Furthermore, data agencies, like Reuters, might be willing to pay for trading data, especially if the exchange facilitates large volumes of trade. Also, if you disseminate all relevant information, an alternative trading mechanism can be set based on your data. For instance, in the United States TRADE is a quote matching system based on the data of the New York Stock Exchange.

Second, disseminating closing price information can have a positive *affect on market behavior.* In general, transparency of trade price information can increase the overall efficiency of the market: without publication of quotes and prices, participants will not have sufficient information to be adequately informed, and the prices of the assets traded in the exchange will not therefore aggregate all available information. As a result, the exchange will not be informationally efficient, and cannot lead to an efficient allocation.

Furthermore, transparency of closing prices can reduce the advantage of informed (inside) traders over pure liquidity traders (e.g. speculators). This has the positive affect of encouraging liquidity providers to trade. Achieving liquidity is the most important goal for any exchange—the "make-or-break" of most e-exchanges, as the next section explains. Furthermore, more trade means more profits for the exchange, since most exchanges charge a percentage or per-trade commission.

WHAT IS LIQUIDITY AND WHO PROVIDES IT?

Liquidity generally refers to how easy it is to transact, i.e. to find a trading partner reasonably quickly. For example, in financial markets a stock is said to be liquid when it can easily and quickly be converted to cash. In practical terms this means that, whatever the price, there will be a buyer for every item sold, and a seller for every item sought. Traders therefore provide liquidity to the exchange. The exchange has enough liquidity if deals get closed quickly, with relatively little effort (in terms of price revisions), and if transaction costs have little impact on trade.

Liquidity is sometimes seen as the "Holy Grail" of electronic exchanges. If the exchange can bring together enough buyers and sellers, then it could work as efficiently and smoothly as the New York Stock Exchange. If, however, the market is not liquid (or "illiquid", or "thin"—to borrow the terms used in financial markets) then traders are less likely to want to trade through it, which in turn will deprive the market of liquidity still further. Moreover, traders who have had a bad experience once are less likely to use the exchange in the future.

To overcome this hurdle, an understanding of who provides liquidity and why is useful. There is an important difference between financial markets and exchanges for "real" commodities, such as steel or cement. In financial markets liquidity is provided by *speculators*. These traders do not produce or consume anything in the traditional economic sense. They simply buy and sell shares to make a profit. Since shares do not take up any physical storage space and do not perish, this is a relatively easy thing to do. However, in markets for physical goods, this is clearly not the case. Since the goods need to be stored, and may perish, liquidity in these markets is provided by intermediaries (or middle-men). In many industries these middle-men are referred to as liquidators. That is, the lack of liquidity in these industries is recognized and profits can, and are, made from it. Sellers facing large storage costs are willing to sell cheap because they cannot find a buyer who is going to actually use the goods. The intermediary then buys the goods, stores them and waits until a buyer desperately in need for the goods cannot get them directly from sellers (because the market is not liquid enough). This buyer will then be willing to pay the intermediary a premium to get the goods now rather than wait.

An understanding of who provides liquidity in the market is essential before attempting to build an exchange. The exchange's chances of succeeding will depend crucially on its ability to attract liquidators and liquidity. The working assumption of many B2B entrepreneurs—that liquidity follows simply by increasing the potential size of the market (by placing it on the web)—has failed too often to be ignored. Quite often traditional industry intermediaries created the more successful exchanges. Fastparts.com—a provider of B2B e-commerce services for the electronic manufacturing industry—is a good example. It was founded in 1991 as an electronic bulletin-board-based trading exchange. In 1996 it launched the first B2B Internet marketplace for buyers and sellers of electronic inventory. It is now a market leader in the provision of B2B e-commerce services in the electronics industry.

Here, buyers and sellers typically comprise original equipment manufacturers, contract electronic manufacturers and component manufacturers and distributors. The main products being traded are capacitors and flash memory, with quantities ranging from one to tens of thousands of units.

Fastpart's aim is to serve the needs of procurement professionals who face the challenges of both excess inventories on cancelled jobs and inventory shortages for unforeseen orders. The creation of its online marketplace helps to improve supply chain efficiencies by allowing companies to buy and sell inventory without disrupting existing sales channels.

As we explained earlier, B2B online transactions have the biggest impact on industries where components and supplies are highly standardized and lend themselves to spot-pricing or auction sales. Databases of such products can easily identify, organize and present comparable information on such product pricing and availability. For each of these products a call auction mechanism can easily be set. Electronic components are thus at the forefront of B2B e-commerce.

For other goods and services the transition to trade through exchanges has been slower. This may change in the years to come. To get from zero to full market liquidity, exchanges need to pass some critical mass point. An exchange that can ensure that some trade will take place through it is therefore more likely to survive. Existing industry consortia, or existing "bricks and mortar" players in the market, are best placed to start these exchanges and quickly achieve liquidity.

Independent exchanges, industry consortia and private networks

Like all trading mechanisms, exchanges make money by charging a per-transaction or percentage fee for successful trade. In addition, they can charge membership fees. However, traders will participate only if their expected gain exceeds these costs. The exchange will therefore need to be able to convincingly answer the following questions.

- What are the average savings the exchange can realistically expect to deliver?
- What will the exchange offer other than savings?
- Are there other exchanges for the same product?

Once the exchange is set up it will want to attract as much liquidity as it can, as quickly as possible. Remember that liquidity attracts liquidity. And the opposite is also true: traders who experience a thin market once may never come back.

A crucial consideration is fairness. *The exchange must be perceived as fair.* The exchange should not prefer buyers to sellers or vice versa. For instance, an exchange that develops from a buyers' club will need to satisfy sellers that they will not be discriminated against. More generally, the exchange should not favor any sub-group of its members. This is particularly important when the owners, or governors, of the market are also traders, such as in Exostar. Finally, the exchange needs to be able to communicate its policy of fairness to potential traders. If fairness cannot be verified, the exchange could suffer.

Existing e-commerce exchanges can be broadly divided into three groups:

1. *independents*, such as RateExchange and Fastparts;
2. *consortia*, such as Converge and Exostar;
3. *private networks*, such as Dell Computer Corporation's e-Marketplace, and Wal-Mart Stores Inc.

Independent exchanges struggle to attract liquidity, since they do not have any themselves. The ones that have survived are those that managed to attract enough liquidity and establish themselves as major players—normally in niche markets for which there is no real alternative.

Industry consortia are doing much better than the independent exchanges. Very few have failed. They normally have enough liquidity to "get going" simply by moving their own trade to the exchange. However, as the Exostar case study in chapter 4 clearly demonstrates, they struggle to convince skeptical non-governing members that their exchange is indeed a fair place to trade. Many of these exchanges are now adopting a very public policy of separating governance from trading activities. In other words, a firm that part-owns the exchange does not receive preferential treatment (e.g. better access to price information). In the case of Converge, for example, which is owned by companies like HP, Dell and Compaq, the exchange is a separate firm with governing members acting as shareholders.

Private networks do not need to convince anyone that they are fair. Clearly they are not, since they are set up and controlled by a single (typically very large) corporation. Whether these networks can become real exchanges will crucially depend on the position of the corporation in the industry. As long as it is sufficiently large compared with the rest, the traders will come. However, it will remain exposed to competition from low-commission independent exchanges, or those set up by a number of smaller competitors in the same industry.

Competition between exchanges

If there are other exchanges for the same product, then they compete. To avoid head-on competition, the exchanges will try to differentiate the services they provide. However, since the exchange also needs to standardize the underlying trading contract, differentiating it might be a problem. There are three broad ways to differentiate.

1. Differentiate by attracting different trader-groups. For example, institutional investors, such as pension funds, are less likely to start trading on a small electronic exchange. In much the same way, exchanges for physical goods can attract different groups.
2. Adopt different trading mechanisms, e.g. a bulletin board versus a call auction.
3. Differentiate through a particular information dissemination policy. An exchange can allow traders to remain anonymous or release more information about closing prices.

In reality, however exchanges compete for the same traders, use similar trading mechanisms and adopt similar information dissemination policies. It is therefore more likely that exchanges will compete head-on, by lowering their commission.

If there are a number of exchanges for the exact same product, then these exchanges essentially compete to attract order-flow (i.e. compete for liquidity). Traders, for their part, seek to minimize costs of trading such as exchange fees, brokerage commissions and the time for the transaction to take place. This implies that exchanges compete by charging less. The trading commission in financial markets in the United States, for example, has fallen considerably in recent years because of competition.

In general, the level of competition will be affected by economies of scale and by network externalities.

Economies of scale arise if the cost per trade declines as the number of trades on the system increases. Such phenomenon will decrease the incentive to compete with the exchange.

Advances in technology have lowered the costs of building trading systems and make the entrance of new entrants easier. Still, some advantages of size do exist.

As for *network externalities*, existing networks and their users have an advantage over potential competitors because order liquidity attracts liquidity; thus, a trading system that already attracts large amounts of orders will have an advantage over any new competing system. However, network externalities can prove to be a disadvantage. For example, if "peak-loading" is a problem, so that the rapidity of the order routing system slows down as the number of orders routed on the system increases, it will be advantageous to use another order routing system if possible.

If more than one exchange is operating, then, unless they always quote the same price, traders can gain by trading on *arbitrage*. Arbitrage is defined as the simultaneous purchase and sale of substantially identical assets in order to profit from a price difference between the two assets. For example, if a bushel of wheat can be bought in one exchange for $3.25, and at another for $4, an investor could guarantee a profit by purchasing wheat in the first exchange and simultaneously selling the same amount on the other exchange. Of course, the price difference must be sufficiently great to offset commissions. Speculators thrive on arbitrage, as do professional investors. The dominant theories of asset pricing (like the Capital Asset Pricing Model, or CAPM) are all based on arbitrage considerations.

One possibility is to ignore this problem: if prices differ, then arbitrage trading is in itself a mechanism to adjust these differences. Alternatively, exchanges may sign agreements that allow them to stop trading if the gaps between prices become very large. Such agreements however can be seen as a first step toward consolidation between the exchanges. If the exchanges are perfectly correlated, then what exactly is their competitive advantage? Overall, this suggests that for most goods and services a single exchange might be the social optimum, as long as the threat of competition is there to keep its commission fees low.

Finally, to protect itself, an exchange should seek to claim as many property rights as possible over the price and quote data it disseminates. We can think of this information as being transmitted "down a wire" from the exchange to the traders. Traders are then not allowed to redistribute the data to other market participants. But how can this be enforced? One strategy is to try to limit the end users as to what they may do with the data. Tokyo Stock Exchange, for instance, insists that vendors deliver its data to their clients on a terminal, as opposed to an electronic data feed that enables redistribution. Many exchanges (e.g. Hong Kong) impose an obligation of confidentiality on the purchaser of their data so as to constrain them from being able to disclose the data without the exchange's permission. Some exchanges impose this obligation also on the end-users of the data, by requiring that an appropriate clause be inserted into a subscriber agreement that the end-user is obliged to sign, or onto their contract with the vendor. However, recent developments in information technology means it is no longer feasible to enforce traders to control the flow of an exchange's data once the trader's digital feed reaches its customers. This makes it very difficult for an exchange to protect its rights over the data. A strategy that rewards traders for loyalty will therefore work better. This goes back to the discussions of optimal incentives provision from chapter 5: if traders are rewarded for loyalty, and if the gains from participating in the exchange are high, then they are less likely to free-ride the exchange information even if the chances of being caught are small.

Final word on incentives

Fairness and liquidity are the main factors determining the decisions of traders whether or not to trade via an exchange. However, these considerations are short-term. In the long run, these decisions are likely to change in response to decisions taken by others. The Neeman–Vulkan (2000) result described in chapter 4 explains these long-run incentives to trade via exchanges.

The more trade takes place via the exchange, the more difficult it becomes for a strong trader to exploit its position outside the exchange. This is because those who are typically "exploited" in direct negotiations, for example buyers who need to sell quickly and consequently cheaply, are better off trading through an exchange (recall from chapter 4 the Morton *et al.* (2001) study, which found that the Internet favors "those who have personal characteristics that put them at a disadvantage in negotiations"). Neeman and Vulkan's result states that in the long run no trade will take place outside an exchange. It the context of this chapter, this result can be thought of as providing a mathematical justification for the argument that "liquidity attracts liquidity", and it reinforces the importance of getting enough liquidity to the exchange as soon as possible.

AUTOMATION

Automation is likely to be a significant factor in the growth of web-based exchanges. Without automation, the costs to traders from participating in an exchange might be too high compared with their trade volume. To participate in an exchange, someone needs to monitor the market price and process the internal information required to determine how much to bid or ask. It is therefore in the interest of the exchange to lower these costs for traders. One way to do this is to provide organizations with automated agents that take care of the day-to-day (or minute-by-minute) trading. A programmable, automated trading agent is essentially costless, apart from the initial time cost of setting it up.

By automating much of the trading process, the exchange is likely to attract more traders, increase its liquidity and therefore become more efficient and profitable overall. However, the success of automation depends crucially on whether users trust software agents to trade on their behalf. Will users trust software agents with such important financial decisions?

The Hewlett–Packard "Jester" experiments provide an excellent example and valuable insights into how agent-based exchanges might work. HP has a general interest in agent technology, and specific interest in automated trading. The company's aim is to understand the reaction of human users to agent interfaces. The motivation for its "Jester" experiments was to examine whether the potential benefits of automated trading were outweighed by problems in human–agent interaction. The aim of the experiment was to engineer a simple scenario in which user reactions to autonomous agents could be investigated.

A group of users of differing backgrounds were presented with a variety of agent and non-agent interfaces under controlled conditions. Of particular interest was the examination of the conceptual model that users form to predict the actions of software trading agents.

Structure of the experiments

An abstract market was created in which buyers and sellers attempted to close deals by the sellers' selling a unit of an abstract product to the buyers. The exchange was based on a call auction market. Buyers and sellers could communicate with each other only through publicly posting bid and offer prices. The market automatically closed any deals where a seller's offer price was less than or equal to a buyer's bid price.

The market was conducted over a series of consecutive trading periods. In any period, each seller could sell at most one unit of the product, while each buyer could buy at most one unit. Each trader was issued with a private reservation price, indicating the cost of the product to sellers or the redemption value to buyers. This was done so that the profit made from the deals could be determined and the subjects rewarded accordingly.

Each trial in the experiment consisted of three such markets run consecutively with the same subjects. In the first market subjects traded manually, directly entering prices to the market. In the second they were required to use a simple agent as a mediator. In the final market subjects could elect one or other interface.

Client interfaces

These included a trading interface, which was either manual or agent, and a web page giving a global view of the state of key market parameters such as the bid–ask spread.

The agents used a trading strategy that responds adaptively to market conditions, i.e. to the publicly available bids and offers. This strategy was used by the agents to periodically adjust the price being shouted in the market. The trading strategy was not however explained to the subjects prior to the experiment.

Users were given control of three agent parameters which they could change at any time:

1. the starting price for the agent to begin negotiating;
2. the limit price, i.e. the upper price limit for buyers' bids to buy and the lower price limit for sellers' offers to sell; users were not compelled to reveal their private reservation prices;
3. a confirmation flag, which allowed the agent either to close the deal itself or to pause while it sought confirmation from the user. (The latter choice obviously ran the risk of losing the deal.)

Experimental results

In comparing the markets when users or agents were trading, the market with agents was found to be much more active. This reflects the differences in trading strategies between users and agents. The human traders were observed to spend more time watching the market and choosing both the timing and the magnitude of price changes. The agents, by comparison, were much more naïve and made smaller, more frequent changes to price. Despite this, however, the market with agent traders converged more closely on the equilibrium price.

Another interesting feature found in the market with agent traders was that there were periodic clusters of off-equilibrium shouts. One possible explanation for this could be that certain users were trying to exercise a lot of control over their agent's behaviour.

When surveyed on the experiment, subjects were asked about the most useful and the weakest features of the agents. A selection of the responses on the most useful features were.

- "It meant I didn't have to think about so many things at once."
- "Freed time to analyze the market."
- "Potential for reacting very quickly to other peoples' shouts."

Comments on the weak features included.

- "I didn't feel in control."
- "Feedback about their strategies, and how these changed over time."
- "It sometimes acted without my instruction, and sometimes disobeyed me!"

These statements provide us with an insight into the strengths and weaknesses of agents as users perceive them. The last comment, for example, indicates that users were trying to build strong conceptual models of the agents. The comment "I didn't feel in control" directly confirms a desire to be in control of the system, and was one of the most frequent negative feedback responses. The next comment underlines the fact that users need to understand their agents' strategies if they are to trust them, since it was assumed by the user that the agent was changing strategy when in fact it wasn't.

In conclusion, evidence supporting both values and pitfalls in using agents to perform tasks emerges from the experiment. There is evidence that agents acting on behalf of their user may be more efficient at the task at hand. However, it also appears that not all users are happy with delegating the responsibility of performing tasks to agents. Users feel that they are no longer in control, despite being able to set the agent's parameters.

The main obstacle to trust is lack of experience of users to trading with agents. If people are given enough time with an agent and can see the benefits of using it, then they are likely to learn to trust it. This, by the way, is true in general, not just for automated agents: people learn to trust their travel agents, accountants, bank managers or secretaries to make decisions on their behalf. The key point is that in the short run agents must be fully transparent, so that users feel "in control".

CASE STUDY

ECNs: Island ECN

Recent technological and regulatory changes have spurred the development of automated trading systems known as electronic communications networks, or ECNs. Advocates of these networks maintain that ECNs will cut transaction costs, speed up trade execution and expand the price information available to investors.

Background: U.S. equity markets

The U.S. equity markets are undergoing significant technological and regulatory changes which could redefine their structure and operation. ECNs have rapidly developed as innovative stock-trading systems that match, buy and sell orders and have captured a sizable share of certain trades.

The stock exchange business amounts to a simple matchmaking enterprise. Matchmakers have traditionally operated in organized exchanges like the New York Stock Exchange (NYSE) and Nasdaq. Here buyers and sellers of securities meet in one central location and execute trades. The NYSE is the largest exchange in the United States with more than 1,366 members. Here there is one matchmaker per stock: the specialist. These specialists enjoy an incredible operating margin of up to 55 percent. On Nasdaq, competing firms known as dealers or market-makers cover each stock. Lacking the specialist's exclusive franchise, these earn more modest, but still substantial, margins of 25 percent.

ECNs first entered the market in the mid-1990s to display and communicate customer buy and sell orders publicly. However they soon developed to match, buy and sell orders directly and thereby came to execute transactions in a way similar to traditional stock exchanges. The networks post the price and size of clients' limit orders (orders to buy or sell specific quantities of a stock at a specified price) and automatically complete transactions internally when appropriate matches are found. If there are no internal matches, the ECNs post the order on the Nasdaq system as soon as it becomes the network's best bid or offer for a stock.

Regulatory developments
The advance of ECNs can be attributed largely to certain regulatory developments in the equity market which helped create a favorable environment for the ECNs.

In 1994, Nasdaq dealers were caught trying to enforce a price-fixing scheme, refusing to execute public limit orders that put forward a better price than they were presenting. In the absence of direct competition from public limit orders, dealers could post lower bid and higher offer prices for stocks and earn excess profits from the wide bid–ask spreads.

However, the Securities and Exchange Commission (SEC) introduced a series of rules culminating in the 1997 order display rule, which ensured that dealers took public limit orders into full account. The new rules require dealers to post such orders on Nasdaq or send them to an ECN to post them. These changes have led to greater transparency and more interaction of limit orders. Since the ECNs' liquidity is based largely on limit order flow, the new rules have encouraged their development.

More importantly, however, the SEC gave ECNs full access to the Nasdaq trading bulletin board. The result is that it now displays all dealers' and ECNs' best prices and quantities. Allowing ECNs onto this system was a crucial change, since beforehand they were able to stay in business only if they could attract both buyers and sellers to form transactions. Once allowed to advertise trades on Nasdaq, however, they need to supply only one party to a transaction—the other can come from anywhere in the Nasdaq system.

Technological advances

ECNs have also evolved naturally from the major advances in telecommunications and computer technology in recent years. They are a natural development following the boom of online brokerage and financial services firms.

There are four main technological advances that have resulted in the rise of ECNs. First, their automated communication and matching systems potentially make trade execution less expensive. By matching buyers and sellers directly, the networks can bypass dealers and thus minimize trading costs by saving them considerable dealer rents.

Swifter trade execution is another possible advantage to ECNs. Their state-of-the-art technology allows them to execute orders much faster than the trading systems of traditional market centers. To illustrate, the turnaround time for an ECN-executed order is 2 to 3 seconds, whereas through an exchange it would be more like 22 seconds.

The third reason is that several ECNs provide investors with more complete price information than traditional market centers. This is because they allow investors to see the network limit order books. An investor with such information is much better placed to assess the market and thus to decide how to place an order.

Finally, by listing only the price and size of an order rather than the trader's identity, ECNs provide traders with anonymity. This is potentially important for informed institutional investors, whose transactions serve as signals to less informed traders.

The recent developments in regulation and technology have led to several ECNs entering the market. Day-trading firms, which for years had sought greater market access to Nasdaq, rushed to set up ECNs. Island ECN, largely owned by the online brokerage Datek, is one example that began handling day-trading orders. Not to be left out, brokerage firms and other traditional players backed their own networks. Strike is an example that was started by Bear Stearns, while REDIBook was launched by the NYSE specialist Spear Leeds & Kellogg. In January 2000 there were nine ECNs registered with the Nasdaq. They have now captured approximately 26 percent of the dollar volume of Nasdaq trading. Their growth rate has been phenomenal, and ECNs have been capturing an additional 1 to 2 percent per quarter.

ECN strategies

The basic formula of ECNs is the same. The networks internally post the size and price of limit orders they get from their clients and automatically execute a trade when a match is found. For example, when a Datek customer places a bid for 500 Microsoft shares at 100, the order is instantaneously sent to Island ECN which scans for a matching seller. If one is found then the trade is automatically completed. If not, the order is posted on Nasdaq as soon as it becomes Island's best Microsoft bid. Once there, anyone with access to Nasdaq can take it.

The ECNs distinguish themselves from one another, however, by targeting different clientele. Some ECNs handle limit orders exclusively, and so orders placed with them do not leave the network until they have been cancelled. Other ECNs take both market orders (orders to buy or sell a stock immediately at the best available price) and limit orders, routing them to the Nasdaq in order to find the best price. For these, if the best price available in the market is through another dealer or network, the ECNs send their orders there.

The networks further differentiate themselves by offering different information to their customers. Some post their limit order books on the web, while others grant individual investors more limited access to price information.

Island ECN

Island is currently the largest ECN and provides an automated trading system for equity securities. Launched in 1997, the network has grown to serve over 350 brokers and executes one out of every eight trades on the Nasdaq. It is now the leading off-exchange trading forum for small investors. On a typical day the company trades over 180 million shares of Nasdaq stock. In the first half of 2000 Island handled trades of more than 23.8 billion shares, worth $1.62 trillion.

Island provides investors with a virtual seat on the trading floor. It is an electronic marketplace that unites buyers and sellers world-wide. Its advantage is that it enables investors to meet directly at the marketplace without having to rely on traditional market intermediaries.

Traditionally, a broker would forward an investor's order to a dealer or specialist in the Nasdaq or NYSE. By placing orders through Island, however, the costs and time-loss linked with operating through middlemen is avoided. Trading through Island has the added advantage of faster execution of trades through its electronic network. It also provides access to research reports, real-time market data, extended trading hours and real-time display of all orders. The company charges only a small per-share percentage fee—approximately $0.75 for every thousand shares traded—rather than the higher percentage-based commission that traditional market-makers charge. It thus seems to offer a comprehensive service to investors while allowing even small ones to be linked to other buyers and sellers world-wide.

How Island works

Investor George enters a limit order to sell 100 shares of Dell at $31.25.

Island's matching engine immediately scans for a match.

George's order is visible to anyone on the
Internet. Since his order is the best offer

for Dell, it is also posted on Nasdaq.
Investor Fred sees George's order and calls

his broker to buy Dell at $31.25.
It's a match.

ECNs or traditional market centers?

Proponents of ECNs argue that they offer substantial
advantages through lower transaction costs, faster execution, providing more information and protecting trader
anonymity. ECNs are also at the forefront of the push
toward after-hours trading. A large proportion of trades—
up to 40 percent—are placed after the market closes,
when investors get home from work; however at the
moment these orders only pile up until the market
reopens in the morning. It is relatively easy for ECNs to
offer extended trading hours as their business is largely

automated and only thinly staffed. Island for example currently trades from 8am to 8pm on weekdays, hoping to capture some of the after-hours business.

However, advocates of traditional market centers maintain that the existence of dealers and specialists results in greater liquidity. The argument is that dealers and specialists supply immediacy by continually standing ready to buy and sell using their own inventory. In contrast, in an automated trading system the buyers and sellers arrive sporadically and so may not find each other immediately. For actively traded stocks, however, the flow of orders itself may be sufficient to supply liquidity and so it is debatable what dealers and specialists could bring to such a market.

Competition or fragmentation?

The entrance of the ECNs into the equity trading market has led to increased competition for trading order flow. There is now more market participation and more competing market centers than ever before. This has already had an effect on the percentages charged to handle orders. The much lower operating margins taken by the ECNs has meant that dealers in traditional markets are having to lower theirs in order to compete. In addition, a study of Nasdaq over the period since the ECNs entered the market shows a narrowing of spreads by an average of 30 percent and dramatic reductions in trading costs. This implies the market is running more efficiently as a result of the increased competition.

Some people however, including the Securities and Exchange Commission (SEC), fear that investors are being hurt by the competing equity trading markets. It is possible that these alternative trading venues are diverting liquidity away from the primary exchanges like the Nasdaq, and that as a result the stock market is becoming more fragmented. The risk of this fragmentation is that it could lead to the pricing of securities varying from one market center to another. The main concern is that markets are not sufficiently linked to create full transparency. This is especially a problem in the on and off-exchange trading of listed stocks. Furthermore, the markets operate at different speeds, which results in price movements at one market center while another is still waiting for confirmation of the trade. With the market becoming fragmented, investors will need to look in several places simultaneously to find the best price—at the Nasdaq listings as well as several ECNs. It is possible that this will be a level of service that only institutions and large retail investors can readily afford.

Lessons from ECNs

- ECNs are a good example of both the opportunities and difficulties in setting web-based exchanges.
- The Internet and the ECNs have significantly reduced the cost to trade, and increased the number of traders and the size and volume of securities markets.
- Intense competition between exchanges has reduced the commission they are able to charge.
- But the long-term prospects of the ECNs are still unclear. On the one hand, arbitrage trading pushes toward more coordination and consolidation between exchanges. On the other hand, exchanges seek to differentiate their offerings, possibly by attracting different types of trader (institutional, day-traders, etc.) in order to reduce the competitive pressure they face.

KEY CONSIDERATIONS FOR E-COMMERCE EXCHANGES
What market participants need to know

- As long as there are many traders in the exchange, there will be no gains from manipulating bids and asks: reporting your true valuation to the exchange may very well be your best strategy.
- If there is more than one exchange for the same product, seek arbitrage opportunities.First, however, ensure that arbitrage trading is still profitable once commissions are considered.
- If the exchange provides you with a software trading agent, it is worthwhile investing the time it takes to train it. In the long run it can save you time and money.

- Part owners of the exchange (for example a member of an industry consortium) should not favor themselves. While they may gain in the short run from doing so, in the long run they will deprive the exchange of liquidity.

What designers need to think about

- Any product or service can be traded in an electronic exchange as long as it can be standardized.
- Standardization is not simple. Even if the product itself is, or can be, standard, issues such as loyalty, reputation and security of long-term contracts are likely to affect the decisions of participants to trade through the exchange.
- Ensure that the product is purchased independently from anything else. If it is not, then consider providing the other products or services that are normally purchased with it.
- Exchanges that set prices reduce negotiation overheads.
- Exchanges that set prices eliminate inefficiencies associated with private information.
- Information regarding the identities of traders needs to be kept private and secret.
- Disseminating closing prices can improve the efficiency of the market.
- Liquidity is essential. Encourage liquidity providers to participate in the exchange.
- Ensure that the exchange delivers savings to participants.
- If there are other exchanges for the same product, then in order to survive the exchange will need to offer either lower commission, or more liquidity, or a differentiated service.
- Industry consortia are the most likely candidates for web-based exchanges, but fairness of trading, in particular between part-owners and others, must be a clear and public policy.
- If there are a number of exchanges for the same product, arbitrage trading can be profitable. Coordination between exchanges can help prevent such trading.

- The exchange needs to protect the information it generates (e.g. closing price information) by whatever legal and technical means possible. If the information can be disseminated easily, than traders can "free-ride" the exchange, by trading directly and not paying commission.
- As for automation, providing traders with software agents can be beneficial. Agents reduce the cost of trading and increase its speed. These effects can increase trading volume, market efficiency and the profits made by the exchange.
- Traders need to trust their agents. The exchange needs to encourage this by making the actions of the agents transparent to users. Also, traders should not be hurried into using such agents.

Bibliography

Akerlof, G., 1970: "The Market for 'Lemons': Quality Uncertainty and the Market Mechanism", *Quarterly Journal of Economics*, Vol. 83(1).

Baye, M.R., and Morgan, J., 2001: "Information Gatekeepers and Competitiveness of Homogeneous Product Markets", *American Economic Review*, Vol. 91(3).

Bertrand, J., 1883: "Theorie mathematique de la richesse sociale", *Journal des savants*.

Binmore, K., 1992: *Fun and Games*, MIT Press, Cambridge, Mass.

Binmore, K., 2000: "Economic Theory Sometimes Works", Discussion Paper, Centre for Economic Learning and Social Evolution (ELSE), University College London.

Binmore, K., and Vulkan, N., 1999: "Applying Game Theory to Automated Negotiation", *Netonomics*, Vol. 1(1).

Brown, J., and Goolsbee, A., 2000: "Does the Internet Make Markets More Competitive? Evidence from the Life Insurance Industry", Working Paper No. 7996, National Bureau of Economic Research.

Brynjolfsson, E., and Smith, M., 2000a: "Frictionless Commerce? A Comparison of Internet and Conventional Retailers", *Management Science*, Vol. 46(4).

Brynjolfsson, E., and Smith, M., 2000b: "The Great Equalizer? Consumer Choice Behaviour at Internet Shopbots", Working Paper, Sloan Business School, MIT.

Bulow J., and Klemperer, P., 1996: "Auctions Versus Negotiations", *American Economic Review*, Vol. 86(1).

Burdett, K., and Judd, K., 1983: "Equilibrium Price Dispersion", *Econometrica*, Vol. 51(4).

Chavez, A., and Maes, P., 1996: "Kasbah: An Agent Marketplace for Buying and Selling Goods", paper presented at the First International Conference on the Practical Application of Intelligent Agents and Multi-Agent Technology, London, April.

Dickinson, I., 1999: "Human Agent Interactions", Technical Report no. 98–130, Hewlett–Packard Laboratories.

The Economist, 2000: "The Container Case", 19 October.

Ernst & Young, 1999: Internet Shopping Survey, available in pdf format: http://www.ey.com/global/vault.nsf/US/Internet_Shopping_Study_1999/$file/internetshopping.pdf

Forrester Research, 2000: "The eMarketplace Shakeout", a TechStrategy report, http://www.forrester.com/ER/Research/Report/Summary/0,1338,10116,FF.html.

Gibbon, E., 1776: *History of the Decline and Fall of the Roman Empire.* London: Strahan and Cadell.

Gibson Research Corporation, 2000: "Homepage": http://grc.com/default.htm

Hotelling, H., 1929: "Stability in Competition", *Economic Journal*, Vol. 39.

Iyer, G., and Pazgal, A., 2002: "Internet Shopping Agents: Virtual Co-Location and Competition", *Marketing Science*, Vol. 22(1).

Jennings, N.R., Farain, P., Johnson, M.J., Norman, T.J., O'Brein, P., and Wiegand, M.E., 1996: "Agent-Based Business Process Management", *International Journal of Co-operative Information Systems*, Vol. 5(2–3).

Klemperer, P., 1999: "Auction Theory: A Guide to the Literature", *Journal of Economic Surveys*, Vol. 13(3).

Klemperer, P., 2001: "What Really Matters in Auction Design", Discussion Paper, Nuffield College, Oxford.

Krulwich, B., 1997: "LifestyleFinder: Intelligent User Profiling Using Large-Scale Demographic Data", *AI Magazine*, Vol. 18(2).

Laseter, T., Long, B., and Capers, C., 2001: "B2B Benchmark: The State of Electronic Exchanges", *Strategy and Business*, issue no. 25.

Lee, R., 1999: *What is an Exchange? The Automation, Management, and Regulation of Financial Markets*, Oxford University Press.

Lucking-Reily, D., 2000: "Auctions on the Internet: What's Being Auctioned, and How?" *Journal of Industrial Economics*, Vol. 48(3).

Milgrom, P., and Roberts, J., 1998: *Economics, Organization and Management*, Prentice-Hall International, Englewood Cliffs, NJ.

Monderer, D., and Tennenholtz, M., 2000: "K-Price Auctions", *Games and Economic Behavior*, Vol. 31(2).

Morton, F.M.S., Zettelmeyer, F., and Silva-Risso, J., 2001: "Consumer Information and Price Discrimination: Does the Internet Affect the Pricing of New Cars to Women and Minorities?" Working Paper no. W8668, National Bureau of Economic Research.

Myerson R., and Satterthwaite M., 1983: "Efficient Mechanisms for Bilateral Trading", *Journal of Economic Theory*, Vol. 29.

Neeman, Z., and Vulkan, N., 2000: "Markets versus Negotiations", mimeo, University College London and Boston University.

Osborn, M., and Rubinstein, A., 1998: *A Course in Game Theory*, MIT Press, Cambridge, Mass.

Reid, A., 2000: "The Face of the Web", on http://www.ipsos-reid.com/US/SERVICES/p_face.cfm

Rodríguez, J.A., Noriega, P., Sierra, C., and Padget, J., 1997: "FM96.5 A Java-based Electronic Auction House", paper presented at the Second International Conference on The Practical Application of Intelligent Agents and Multi-Agent Technology: (PAAM '97), London.

Roth, A., 1990: "New Physicians: A Natural Experiment in Market Organization", *Science*, issue no. 250.

Roth, A., and Ockenfels, A., 2000a: "Last Minute Bidding and the Rules for Ending Second-Price Auctions: Theory and Evidence from a Natural Experiment on the Internet", Working Paper, Harvard Business School; forthcoming in *American Economic Review*.

Roth, A., and Ockenfels, A., 2000b: "Last-Minute Bidding and the Rules for Ending Second-Price Auctions: Evidence from eBay and Amazon Auctions on the Internet", forthcoming in *American Economic Review*.

Rubinstein A., 1982: "Perfect Equilibrium in a Bargaining Model", *Econometrica*, Vol. 50(1).

Rustichini, A., Satterthwaite, M., and Williams, S., 1994: "Converges to Efficiency in a Simple Market with Incomplete Information", *Econometrica*, Vol. 62(5).

Sandholm, T., and Vulkan, N., 2000: "Bargaining with Deadlines", *Proceedings of the National Conference on Artificial Intelligence (AAAI)*, Orlando, Fla: AAAI.

Shapiro, C., and Varian, H., 1999: *Information Rules*, Harvard Business School Press, Boston.

Sierra C., Faratin P., and Jennings N.R., 1997: "A Service-Oriented Negotiation Model between Autonomous Agents", paper presented at a conference on the Practical Applications of Intelligent Agents and Multi-Agent Technology (PAAM), organized by Practical Applications.

Streitfeld, D., 2000: "On the Web, Price Tags Blur", *Washington Post*, 27 September.

Ulph, D., and Vulkan, N., 2000a: "Electronic Commerce and Competitive First degree Price Discriminators", Discussion Paper, University College, London.

Ulph, D., and Vulkan, N., 2000b: "E-Commerce, Mass Customization and Price Discrimination", Discussion Paper, University College, London.

Varian, H., 1980: "A Model of Sales", *American Economic Review*, Vol. 70(4).

Vulkan, N., 1999: "Economic Implications of Agent Technology and E-commerce", *The Economic Journal*, February 1999.

Vulkan, N., 2001: "Equilibria for Automated Negotiations", *Games and Economic Behavior*, Vol. 35(1–2).

Vulkan, N., 2002: "Strategic Design of Mobile Agents", *Artificial Intelligence Magazine*, Vol. 23.

Vulkan, N., and Jennings, N., 2000: "Efficient Mechanism for Service Allocation in Multiagent Systems", *Decision Support Systems*, Vol. 28(1–2).

Index

WITHDRAWN